Advance praise for Honeycomb Kids

One world. One humanity. One destiny. It can all start with one family: yours. Honeycomb Kids *gives you the ideas and tools you need to parent with the future in mind.*

PROFESSOR TIM FLANNERY

Sustainable lifestyles and families lead to real wealth. Use this book to help you start investing now.

DAVID WANN, AUTHOR, *SIMPLE PROSPERITY*

Anna Campbell's 'honeycomb' is a metaphor for a context in which parents can raise resilient, capable, caring kids who can make their way in, and contribute positively to, a world that currently appears to be careening toward environmental and economic ruin. Parents who are aware of climate change, peak oil, and other global problems will find both honesty and inspiration.

RICHARD HEINBERG, AUTHOR, *THE END OF GROWTH*,
SENIOR FELLOW, POST CARBON INSTITUTE

We face a pressing challenge of creating resilient communities able to meet the challenges of peak oil, climate change and over consumption. Honeycomb Kids *provides an easy-to-read, handy tool for shaping a sustainable, fulfilling future. While it provides practical ideas for how to nurture children who focus on what really matters, it also challenges parents and community members to reconsider how* **we** *live. Hopefully it will generate conversations* *and action at dinner tables, schools, playgroups, places of worship, parties and even boardrooms throughout the country.*

DR GRAEME STUART, FAMILY ACTION CENTRE,
THE UNIVERSITY OF NEWCASTLE

Positive change in the world comes about with the rise of new generations, so this guide for parents helping children grow through both global and personal challenges is both needed and very welcome.

TIM COSTELLO, CHIEF EXECUTIVE, WORLD VISION AUSTRALIA

Honeycomb Kids *provides an important and timely contribution to the 'collective wisdom' of modern day parents across the globe. It is unique in its approach and scope, addressing parenting and child development in the context of wider society and the significant and unprecedented changes that are taking place, both locally and worldwide.* Honeycomb Kids *presents a convincing argument for reconnecting modern-day children with nature, family and community, which moves way beyond the individual, and explores the impact of doing so (and not doing so) on future generations, and the health of the planet. This book has something for everyone and just like life itself, offers light and shade, humour and deeper contemplation, frustration and hope. Full of practical suggestions (to which we are kindly encouraged to "add our own special ingredients") and honest reflection, this mother's journey offers sincerity and inspiration and is set to be an important catalyst for affecting change, for the betterment of families, communities and humankind.*

LENORA NEWCOMBE, PRESIDENT OF HUNTER ALLIANCE FOR
CHILDHOOD INC.

If you're a parent or a grandparent wondering how to tread lightly into the 21st century, you might like to start by reading this book.

KIRSTY MCKENZIE, EDITOR, *AUSTRALIAN COUNTRY COLLECTIONS*

Read it yourself, be inspired, and give it as a gift to anyone you know with children—the planet will thank you!

PETER DRISCOLL, CO-FOUNDER, TRANSITION SYDNEY

HONEYCOMB KIDS

Big-picture parenting
for a changing world

...and to change the world!

Anna M Campbell

Published by

Cape Able
Self Reliance. Sustainability. Discovery

2012

Published by Cape Able
First published in Australia in 2012
By Cape Able Publishing
ABN: 44081882064
www.capeable.com

National Library of Australia Cataloguing-in-Publication entry:

Author: Campbell, Anna M. 1969- .

Title: Honeycomb Kids: Big-picture parenting for a changing world...and to change the world!

ISBN 978-0-9807475-0-8
Subjects: Parenting
             Child rearing.
Dewey Number: 649.1

Cover design: Cathi Stevenson

Cover images: Honeycomb image: ©iStockphoto.com/Ryan Burke. Image of family: ©iStockphoto.com/Ace_Create

Interior design: 1106 Design

Printed by Thomson-Shore

Dedication

·····························

Well of course this is dedicated to you ☺

Contents

Introduction

*Inspiration is not garnered from the litanies of what may
befall us; it resides in humanity's willingness to restore,
redress, reform, rebuild, recover, reimagine, and reconsider.*
PAUL HAWKEN, 2009 COMMENCEMENT SPEECH
AT THE UNIVERSITY OF PORTLAND

*What lies behind us and what lies before us are
tiny matters compared to what lies within us.*
RALPH WALDO EMERSON

There's honeycomb and then there's honeycomb. The stuff you buy in a chocolate bar is an unhealthy factory mix of preservatives, synthetic colour and refined sugar, but the real golden yellow network of honeycomb produced by honey bees is one of nature's wonders. It's a thing of beauty, strength, utility, nutrition, healing, sweetness and longevity. It's the product of a community working together for the benefit of all with the past in mind, the present in hand and future needs constantly factored in.

One cell of honeycomb won't keep even a single bee alive, but when the cells are joined together and filled with nectar and pollen, they provide individual bees and the colony with a strong, resilient, bounteous framework in which they can thrive.

1

That's why this book is called *Honeycomb Kids*. It's all about working to build this kind of resilience within your own family and community, and providing a framework in which your children will thrive, both now and in the future.

The honeycomb approach to childraising actually makes parenting a whole lot easier, and loads more fun too! It does this by enabling families to see the big picture, to set a clear direction, to focus on what really matters in life and to go against the tide of consumerism at all costs. It's about empowering our kids, rather than just driving them around.

Let's say you saw a vicious dog chasing your neighbour's child; you'd run to intercept it. If you saw a drunken person scaring kids at the shops, you'd shepherd the children to safety. If you saw your own child racing onto a busy road to retrieve a ball, you'd shout a warning.

We act quickly and decisively when we see an immediate threat to our children's welfare, yet many of us tend to avoid even thinking about longer-term threats, or opportunities for that matter.

Let's face it; our days can be such a whirlwind that thinking about and acting on the strategies and tactics that will really help our children in the long term is often put in the too-hard basket. We spend so much time preparing them for ballet concerts and weekend sporting finals, but hardly any time at all preparing them for the real world.

Since my own family made some tough decisions and started living "honeycomb style," our lives have become a lot more enjoyable, economical and environmentally friendly. I reckon we're more fulfilled, calmer, and content and, funnily enough, more comical! Though I have to admit, the comical part ain't all that hard when there are three children under twelve!

We realised that rather than a bigger TV, we needed a bigger viewpoint. And that rather than a bigger house, we needed a bigger life. Instead of swarming to the shops, we now swarm into the world.

A few years into focusing on the big picture, we find ourselves less distracted as parents, more adept at decision-making, more open to adventure and less blinded by bling. Our children's personalities, skills and community-mindedness are blossoming, and our sense of health, happiness, community and personal wellbeing is stronger than ever.

That's not to say we're a perfect family; far, far from it. We still yell, raise hell, waste too much and want too much. We can be selfish and short-tempered, unfocused, greedy, closed-minded and grumpy. We also tantrum and bribe and let things slide...but hey; we used to be much worse!

The idea behind *Honeycomb Kids* is simple: to raise resilient, capable, caring kids (who in turn will become resilient, capable, caring adults), we need to take a flight outside our hive and take in the surrounding view. It's about looking at a jigsaw puzzle as a whole, rather than the piece right in front of us. It's about raising our kids in the context of the planet, and the next hundred years, not in the context of our lounge room and the next ad break.

MORE THAN ONE WAY TO LIVE

During the past five years our family has made a huge shift in our lifestyle. We did that by:

- committing to spend more time communicating than commuting
- focusing our attention on community rather than consumption
- striving to generate less waste while making room for more wisdom
- accepting less income, but better outcomes
- achieving more self-reliance and therefore less dependency.

These are five simple areas of focus that any family, living in any city, suburb or regional area can adopt.

It's funny that, although we Westerners are happy to spend hours researching the best of 100 mobile phone plans or 40 different types of breakfast cereal or choosing between a million different shelving options in an Ikea store, we rarely even consider that there's more than one way we can CHOOSE TO LIVE!

Well, there certainly is more than one way to live, and definitely more than one way to parent.

The other night, my husband and I were talking about life, death and the whole shebang, and we finally crystallised what would give us peace on our (hopefully very, very far-off) deathbed. It was simply the knowledge that our children and our children's children would be capable, resilient and robust; that they'd be able to work within themselves and with people in their community to find a way through; that they'd find creative, compassionate solutions to the problems they came up against.

That legacy is what we're working on in our family right now, and that's why I've written this book. It's the one I desperately wanted to read, but couldn't find in a bookstore anywhere. Yes, there have been a gazillion books written about disciplining children and creating happy families, and almost as many on peak oil, climate change and survival skills, but we were just never able to find one that brought them together, and addressed our own goals, dreams and concerns for our children and the very different hive they may end up living in.

This book is for our kids, your kids and all the children who will be living on the planet with them and after them, because I truly believe that by preparing for tomorrow, we can all enjoy life a whole lot more today. And you know what? Parenting with a road map, with a destination in mind, with the big-picture view, makes parenting a WHOLE lot easier. It makes it easier to avoid distractions; it makes it easier to say "no" and for that "no" to stay no rather than giving in to pester power; and it also makes it easier to laugh, easier to love, and easier to grow.

OUR SHIFT

That's the journey our family are on. If you'd told me six years ago that I'd be taking care of three children, three horses, eight alpacas, eight cows, 12 goats, 30 sheep, 50 chickens, 20,000 worms, 400,000 bees and a hillside full of plants of importance to humanity, I would have laughed and handed you a straitjacket.

I think my parents wanted to hand me the same straitjacket when my husband and I told them we were giving up our well-paid white-collar city jobs to head for the country. But finding some 'real' space, learning new skills and living more sustainably became a magnet to us. We felt an urgency to get back in touch with nature, to see the sky rather than skyscrapers, to connect with creatures rather than concrete, to let our kids run free rather than be run by schedules...to bake bread rather than simply unwrap it.

Since then we've hosted more than 2,000 children and their parents, scores of WWOOFers (willing workers on organic farms), and coachloads of visitors on our farm, learning alongside them the ways of nature, farming, self-reliance, self-sufficiency, natural health, solar cooking and sharing. It's been quite a journey! It's been humbling, inspiring and loads of fun.

Of course, you don't need to change your location to experience these changes in your family; changing your mind-set is what it's all about.

Not all of us want to live in the country. That's why the ideas in this book can be applied to the townhouse, the penthouse, the farmyard, the courtyard, the suburban shack and the granny flat. You see, no matter where you live in your little world, you're part of a much bigger one. There are about seven billion humans sharing the planet right now, and the impact of this growing population on our children will be immense.

This is where honeycomb parenting comes in. It's about thinking on a broad scale about things like the environment, society, health, economics, politics, personal growth, threats and opportunities, and using that knowledge to empower our children so that 10, 20, 30 years from now, they're in a great position to rise above, and be part of, the solution to many of the inevitable problems on the horizon.

In the West we have our cars, infinite appliances and 20 types of cake mix, but we also now have—for starters—financial meltdowns, firestorms, terrorism, a rise in mental illness[1], water shortages, an ever-increasing cost of living and volatile oil prices. In developing nations near and far away, there's not a lot of cake mix going around, but there are a huge number of things being stirred up that will affect our children's futures.

Like a lot of people, I used to sit around on the couch wondering what it would be like to win the lottery, get that pay rise, buy that big house. But you can't buy resilience with a lottery ticket. Capability doesn't come in a scratchie. A pay rise doesn't help us rise above.

For years, I was so busy and distracted I never questioned the treadmill our family was on, the role we played in society, or how our society might change during the course of our children's lives. I was more of a TV-picture parent than a big-picture parent. Our debt kept growing larger, our working days kept getting longer and it became ever so easy to fill what little spare time we had with after-school activities, TV programs, car trips to the shops and pre-packaged treats. Our lives were full to bursting rather than full as in fulfilling. Though we could have everything we wanted—or so it felt, thanks to the credit card—we realised we couldn't actually

---

[1] The World Health Organisation in 2001 estimated that approximately 450 million people worldwide have a mental health problem. Additionally, the 2007 National Survey of Mental Health and Wellbeing conducted by the Australian Bureau of Statistics found that an estimated 3.2 million Australians (20 per cent of the population aged between 16 and 85) had a mental disorder in the 12 months prior to the survey. The UK's Mental Health Foundation states that the rate of self-harm in Great Britain is the highest in all of Europe.

DO anything! And although we bought and consumed a lot, we didn't really produce a lot or give a lot back.

We were so easily distracted by electronic entertainment and consumption that we weren't focusing on nurturing in ourselves (or our children!) the skills, tools, traits, knowledge and curiosity that would be useful throughout a lifetime.

So what were the triggers for changing our lives? There were definitely a few...I can remember the horror of September 11 playing out on our TV screen, and I can remember my interest being piqued when I heard for the first time about Peak Oil and how the supply and price of oil makes all of us in Western nations so vulnerable. I remember reading through the list of ingredients on a bottle of our children's shampoo, and then looking them up to find out what they actually were, and being shocked. And I remember standing in the hospital while the doctors stared at my husband's purple, bloated legs and announced that it was probably sarcoidosis, most likely caused by exposure to chemicals. There were other triggers too, like realising I didn't really know anything about the basics of growing food and that I was pretty much useless unless I was attached to a computer keyboard. These triggers have since led us on a journey of discovery to a life that feels safer and yet 100 times more thrilling than the life we lived before.

It doesn't take news broadcasts to inform us that our world is facing immense challenges. The impact of these challenges will be fully felt by our children's generation, and that's why the time is right to refresh our life and parenting philosophy with ideas and concepts that will stand our children in good stead for their entire lifetimes, disasters or no disasters, climate change or climate the same, prosperity or paucity. And it's all about empowering them. A meaningful, joyous childhood—and therefore adulthood—is reliant on exposing them (and ourselves!) to ideas, actions, knowledge, wisdom and skills, and not just academic or sporting skills, but problem-solving skills and life skills that will be useful to them and their wider community long after they have outgrown their soccer boots and their Maths coach.

OUR QUEST

There's something so romantic and evocative about the word 'quest'. It's like something out of an olden-days adventure. And although we are not the Knights of the Round Table, we are all the Knights of our own Kitchen Tables, and it's around them we can dream and make plans for living the best life we can. Then we can get up from those tables and put those big ideas into action.

For a few years, it seemed like my role in life was just to keep it all together long enough to get home from work, de-stress in front of the TV and then do it all again the next day. But that soon got old, and forced our family to get bold.

Living every day with a sense of purpose means that little problems and temptations are unable to throw us off course for long or bring us down too low. A quest gives us the strength to overcome rather than be overcome. Quests can be little or they can be large, it's just important to go on one!

My quest right now revolves around the welfare of our children, the planet they live on and the people and creatures we share it with. It's not a boring quest or a tough quest, indeed it's actually quite exhilarating, but I'd be lying if I didn't tell you I started on this quest not from some great sense of compassion, but out of a sense of fear and foreboding. But hey, we've all gotta start somewhere and it doesn't matter where; it's where we end up that counts! And the good news is: the more you discover, the more compassionate you become anyway!

I used to think that the queen bee directed the worker and drone bees, but I've since learned she doesn't. Each individual bee is able to give input and then the hive as a whole decides on the most meritorious ideas and actions to implement. It's a true democracy. And that's how I hope you approach this book. There are as many different ways to beekeep as there are to parent, so of course, you're not going to agree with everything written within these pages. What I really hope is that you discover a honeycomb of ideas and concepts to help your family start a dialogue, an imagining, and an alternative and adventure-filled road map to life as we don't know it!

WHAT KIND OF WORLD WILL OUR KIDS INHERIT?

Don't you love how life before kids was so simple? We didn't need to dwell on what to cook for dinner, a weekly wash took care of the laundry and the only arguments we had were about where to go on holiday.

Then we have children, and suddenly we have responsibility, feeding schedules, three loads of washing a day and amped-up arguments with militant midgets. But somehow this dazzling love kicks in, and we know we'd do anything to help our children not only survive but thrive.

And it's because of that huge love that we realise that, even with the big-screen TV, the huge array of food available to us in the supermarket, the distraction of work, the rush of after-school activities and all the options for play, we know something isn't quite right. There's this little bit of anxiety that keeps bubbling up in the back of our minds.

I'm here to tell you that there's a good reason for that anxiety, and ignoring it won't make it go away!

To future-proof our kids, we need to take the world view rather than the suburban view; we need to put our focus on panoramic rather than zoom. Now, more than ever, we parents need to listen, question, research, discover and probe. It's about taking a fresh look at all the things we've always done, always bought, always believed, and seeing if they're still relevant and optimal given what we now know about the world.

When I think about the kind of world our children will inherit, there are really only two choices:
- a better one
- a more challenging one.

Let's explore these options some more (the good news first, of course!).

THE SHINY CRYSTAL BALL—A BETTER WORLD

Let's start with a crystal-ball vision for a better world:

Yes, a better world is certainly within reach for our children. It's a world that is fairer, kinder, safer, less polluted, more connected, more hopeful, more peaceful. It's more bounteous for all. By taking less, we've discovered that we end up with more of what truly adds to our happiness. It's a world of optimism and compassion, where leisure time and great art thrive and inventions and technology work for the masses.

It's a world of healing, of shared futures. It's a world where decisions aren't made based on a quarterly profit report to the stock market or on short political terms, but on outcomes that will affect the wellbeing of the planet and humanity over centuries. It's a world where people become true caretakers of each other and of the Earth; its diversity, its species, its natural resources.

Instead of war, peace breaks out! Humanity decides that war is not a solution, so all conflicts cease. As Mahatma Gandhi said, "There is no way to peace. Peace is the way." Your children have no fear of 'them' or 'others', but embrace and accept people of different cultures, heritage and religions. They understand the connectedness of all humans. Defence spending, a huge portion of national budgets until now, has been diverted to bring all peoples around the world out of poverty.

A concerted and successful effort by governments the world over has led to the provision of education and opportunities for "those left behind". Many of the main drivers of conflict have been disempowered.

Your children are reaping the benefits of years of scientific and medical research that means a healthier life for all. Government budgets were revised years ago to focus on preventative medicine solutions, rather than medicine for the sick, and this has made a huge difference in your children's lives, giving them healthy longevity. Money no longer needed for treating an ailing population has been spent on research and produced excellent results in treating previously untreatable diseases.

Your children are part of a generation that grew up understanding the importance of teamwork and responsibility, and the benefits of strong communities.

You brought them up to do good, not just well. They never spent years of their lives in front of the TV, playing video games or abusing substances. Instead, they were out having fun, being contributors, feeling good about themselves and making a difference.

Your children have ridden the wave of a more efficient and less emissive energy generation. They may even work in the solar, wind or hydrogen industries. You don't need to worry about the health of their lungs, kidneys or livers, because the air and water is the cleanest it has been in centuries.

Your children live productive and fulfilling lives. They've been part of the generation that insisted on reducing the gap between the world's richest and poorest, thus healing many of the problems of our own day.

Your kids sure know how to balance work and play, community and career, family and friends, responsibilities and pleasures. Gone are the long commutes, the endless hours spent in unfulfilling jobs, the time away from family. They've followed their interests, made time for their relatives (including you in your old age) and their friendships are strong and sound.

Your children live in a society that has eagerly and voluntarily reduced its consumption of material goods, chemicals and processed foods. They and their peers have ensured that the earth can replenish itself and continue to provide. Your children support urban food growing and farming that builds the soil, rather than stripping it. Daily they enjoy fresh, healthy, locally grown, sustainable produce. They even have you over for dinner to show off their gardening and cooking skills! You're 80 now, and they actually invite you to move in with them so you can share even more fun meals and times together! Your grandkids can't help you unpack your bags fast enough.

Your children fulfil their potential through studying, travelling, being mentored, apprenticed and guided. They benefit physically and mentally from being given the time to follow the path of their choosing, to explore, to navigate, to discover, invent and share.

Your children have no hesitation bringing their own children into the world, because it is a peaceful, beautiful, balanced and bounteous one. This is what we would wish for generations to follow.

But there are looming threats to this ideal world, and if we don't factor them into our parenting, we're parenting in a vacuum. Writing in *Brain, Child* magazine, Tracey Mayor summed up parenting in a changing world well when she asked, "What if we're raising our kids to succeed in a George Jetson kind of world, but they wind up living more like Fred Flintstone?"

THE CLOUDY CRYSTAL BALL—THE REALITY OF A BLEAKER WORLD

It's definitely unnerving and upsetting to discover that the life most Westerners lead might be at risk and, if the truth be told, isn't actually fair or healthy for the bulk of humanity anyway.

Many of us want to think, "Everything's fine, things won't change for our kids," because it enables us to continue to live as we're used to. But by acknowledging that the future might not be so rosy, and that our current society isn't perfect, we're given the chance to keep the best of it while fixing the broken stuff. I mean, just because we ignore the elephant in the room doesn't mean it isn't there, and who wants an elephant suddenly sitting on their kids unannounced?!

By knowing the dangers and risks at a personal, local and global level, we can find comfort in working to avoid or at least minimise their impact. And we can also maximise the good stuff too! It's like when you're caring for a beehive, if you don't know the potential of how different pests, diseases and weather conditions can affect the hive, you can't avoid them or nurture and build up the hive's natural defences to withstand and survive them.

And there are a few issues our earthly hive is already being forced to deal with. For starters:

A cursory glance reveals that just like the honeycomb structure of a beehive, all these issues are connected. Unfortunately, that makes them even tougher to deal with.

In Kim John Payne's book, *Simplicity Parenting,* he writes, "When we act out of reverence instead of fear, our motivation is stronger, our inspiration boundless," which is so true. And yet, sometimes I think we need a little fear or perceived sense of loss to actually appreciate what we have, and to develop that reverence. It's like the person who rediscovers life after a serious illness; you see and act quite differently when you've taken in the big picture. When you're aware of the big picture, it also helps you develop the compassion needed to make a difference in the world. That's because once you know what's going on "out there", hopefully you will want to help alleviate the suffering of not just your immediate family, but your wider community and future generations.

The next section covers some of these big issues in more detail, while the second half of the book offers up a wide variety of ideas and actions that will help you equip your children with the headspace, knowledge, skills and lightness to help them 'do' and 'feel' their best as adults in this changing world.

Part 1:
The Big Issues

In his book, *Ecological Intelligence*, Daniel Goleman writes:

"Our brains are exquisitely attuned to pinpoint and instantly react to a fixed range of dangers…Nature hard-wired the brain's alarm circuitry to spot and recoil immediately from objects hurtling toward us, threatening facial expressions, snarling animals, and like dangers in our immediate physical surroundings. That wiring helped us to survive to the present.

"But nothing in our evolutionary past has shaped our brain for spotting less palpable threats like the slow heating of the planet, the insidious spread of destructive chemical particulates into the air we breathe and things we eat, or the inexorable destruction of vast swaths of flora and fauna on our planet….Our brain excels at handling threats in the moment but falters at managing those coming at us in some indefinite future."

Here are some of those threats:

POPULATION GROWTH

The place is getting a bit crowded, don't you think? One hundred years ago, the world's population was less than two billion. Twelve years ago it was six billion. At the time of writing it's seven billion. And all the while we've been mining, chomping, chewing, sawing, building on and burning through the Earth's natural resources and species at a great rate. And the most alarming thing is that you may not have even noticed or cared! You might not see all that many people on your street at home, but we're out there, and global competition for natural resources is coming to a head.

CLIMATE CHANGE

Water scarcity, food shortages, inundation of low-lying areas, tropical diseases, drought and volatile weather patterns could lead to mass migration and immeasurable suffering, not to mention the resulting financial drain leading to lower living standards around the world. Depending on where your children choose to live as adults, the weather they experience may become calmer or more calamitous, milder or wilder. Climate change, carbon taxes, insurance costs, droughts, floods, tornadoes, cyclones, fires and storms have a lot in store for our children.

Natural Disasters

The world has always experienced natural disasters. Some cities are used to their regularity, while others are utterly unprepared. Some have forgotten the history of their lands, while some lands seem to be creating new history. Over the past few years, satellites have regularly beamed pictures to our TVs of disasters from all corners of the globe. When these are pixelated on the flat screen, we can never really feel the horror, the pain and the loss of the people who are directly affected. The 2009 Victorian bushfires burned across 330,000ha (815,000 acres) of southern Australia, caused the deaths of more than 170 people and incinerated more than 2,000 dwellings. In August 2005 Hurricane Katrina swept in from the Gulf of Mexico and caused the deaths of at least 1,836 people, nearly $US90 billion in property damage and national hand-wringing at the slow and uncoordinated recovery effort. There was a steady stream of disasters in 2011 too, from the Mississippi River and Queensland floodings to the earthquake in Christchurch, New Zealand to the tornadoes in the US, and the largest of them all, the earthquake, tsunami and nuclear emergency in Japan, which rolled three disasters into one. In all of these incidents, many felt let down by the warnings and advice of their governments. Though many people acted heroically and did the best they could, it was obvious that just as many were unprepared, totally caught off-guard by the sheer ferocity and longevity of the situation they found themselves swept up in. Earthquakes, fires, floods, famines, pestilence, volcanoes, tornadoes, mudslides, tsunamis, avalanches and typhoons… simply listing them doesn't do the suffering justice. I don't want my kids waiting for help that doesn't come. I want them to be able to help themselves and others. The devastating floods in Queensland early in 2011 showed the interconnectedness and knock-on effects of nature's fury, with coal supplies disrupted and food crops wiped out, but they also showed the valiant nature of complete strangers who pitched in to help with the clean-up.

FOOD SHORTAGES

If you live in a developed country, you've probably never gone a day without food in your life, unless you were fasting for an operation or being 'cleansed' at a fancy retreat! Food, a huge variety of it, is available 24 hours a day at our local shopping centres. We have so much that it's hard to shut our cupboards sometimes, or to make room in the fridge. But will it be the same in the future? Can our world continue to provide for the West's insatiable appetite for food to the level to which most of us have been accustomed? Should it? And will our own families one day have difficulty affording it? Food shortages, volatile prices and less choice will definitely mean that your children's tables will never again be so laden so inexpensively, so constantly, with so much choice and certainly with so little effort on their part. The dramatic plunge in the world's fish stocks[2], droughts and floods affecting global crop supplies, pestilence, the increasing cost of oil for pesticides, fertilisers and transport, depleted soils, poor farming practices and an extra 100 million babies each year to feed can only lead to food shortages and further inequity of distribution. That's even before we factor in the collapse of bee colonies around the world, bees that we rely on to pollinate 40 per cent of our food supply.

WATER SCARCITY

All around the world, aquifers are being tapped and depleted at an extraordinary pace as humans become more and more reliant on groundwater, and as droughts and increased evaporation of surface water occur. Increasing population and industrial demand have driven the consumption of water higher, and old infrastructure in many major cities leads to increasing waste. Mexico City has sunk by a whopping 11 metres (36 feet) in the past century as its residents drink, wash and irrigate their way through their underground water supply. Then there is the proliferation of desalination plants in coastal cities, chewing up energy to turn salt water into fresh, and coal seam gas mining processes and pollutants changing underground water forever. In the West, unless we live near coal seam gas extraction activities or downriver from an industrial area, we've hardly had to think about the health of our water. If you didn't like the taste of the water in your area, or wanted to avoid fluoride or other additives, you just bought bottled water or a filter. But according to the non-profit organisation The Water Project, at any one time, half the world's hospital beds are occupied by patients suffering from waterborne diseases. We in the West have been incredibly lucky, but that luck hasn't been shared by the rest

---

[2] If current trends continue, scientists predict that the world's fisheries could completely collapse by 2050. Worm, et al. (2006) "Impacts of biodiversity loss on ocean ecosystem services." Science, 314 (5800), p. 787.

of humanity. The third edition of the United Nations World Water Development Report, released on March 16, 2009, states that "it is clear that urgent action is needed to avert a global water crisis… leading to political insecurity and conflict at various levels." Where I live, it goes from flood to drought quicker than you can put up your umbrella. Thirty years from now, there will be even more demand for water, and our children will need to know how to capture it, conserve it, store it and make the most of it.

ENERGY SUPPLY

We flick on a switch and lights bathe even the darkest room. We open our freezer to find a veritable feast. We turn on the shower and warm water pours over us. We're feeling hot so we use a remote control to switch on a fan or an airconditioner. We drive to work, and traffic signals enable the safe transit of thousands of vehicles. Should we run one of those lights and have a terrible accident, a machine breathes for us. We are so reliant on electricity that a few hours without it cause angst and frustration. How would you cope if your power didn't come back on for a day, or a week, or a month? The demands on ageing systems caused by large populations running all manner of devices, the demands on the environment caused by the pollutants being belched from coal-powered plants, and the demands on people attempting to meet the rising cost of their power usage will continue to surge. For those who can still afford electricity, major blackouts will occur—and they'll probably occur more often thanks to increasing demand, crumbling infra-structure, and damage and disruption caused by extreme weather events. It makes sense to acknowledge the limitations of our current infrastructure, and the extent of our reliance upon it.

Peak Oil: Oil Price & Supply Vulnerability

No other substance is as critical to today's world as oil. Everything you and I do relies on its use. Its importance cannot be underestimated, and nothing—not solar, not gas, not hydrogen—can replace all its functions. That's a huge worry, because oil is concentrated in so few hands, reserves are rapidly depleting, and the oil that's left is becoming more difficult and more expensive to extract. The International Energy Agency's (IEA) chief economist Fatih Birol finally announced in 2011 that they believe the world's crude oil production peaked in 2006, many years earlier than they had previously estimated. That means there is now less oil in the ground than has already been extracted. It's a tipping point. The world is addicted to oil, and that's why not even a year after 2010's Deepwater Horizon oil disaster, plans were afoot to carve up the Arctic in search of more of the black gold. Think about it... our families will never have any control over either its price or its supply. Most of the countries where it can be found don't really like "us". The wars waged to get it eat it up at an even faster rate. And yet, it remains the commodity solely responsible for food production, transport, energy, mining, plastics and pharmaceuticals, as well as being used at some stage in the production line of all the renewable fuels such as solar panels, hydrogen, biogas and biodiesel. Our societies only run the way they run because of oil. Oil enables ambulances to come to our rescue, workers to get to power stations, buses to take the elderly to grocery stores, trucks to transport building supplies and food...and so, so much more. It's worth preparing our children for a world where cheap, abundant oil is no longer the reality. We need to wean ourselves off it, finding alternative ways to live our lives, or the cost of oil, its shortages and the wars it leads to will see instability and dislocation dominating our children's adult years. As Richard Heinberg of the Post Carbon Institute said, "...continued appeals to wishful thinking merely squander opportunities to pre-adapt gracefully and painlessly to a lower-energy future."

Peak Metals

Like Peak Oil, the theory of Peak Metals deals with the depletion and growing scarcity of the minerals and metals that are used in countless everyday items, and their rising cost as demand outstrips supply. A decade ago, no one envisaged the price of copper would rise so high that thieves would steal taps from schools, copper plaques from cemeteries and copper wire from railway signal poles. Imagine walking along a city street and falling into a sewer because someone has stolen the grates and manholes to sell at the scrap metal yard! Well, it's already happening! Tauranga City Council in New Zealand had 19 stormwater grates stolen in a single night in November 2010. Cambridgeshire County Council in the UK reported the theft of 38 gulley grates over a fortnight in March 2011 and the FBI reported back in 2008 how the theft of copper wire in Polk County, Florida left 4,000 residents without power. Then there are the elements that only school science whizzes would remember, but that now help us to lead the lifestyles we take for granted, like indium and gallium. Indium is used in the production of solar cells, the windows of aeroplanes and trains, LCD screens, and in nuclear medicine, for starters. Gallium is also used in solar cells, as well as in mobile phones and electronics applications. In 2010, headlines were made around the world when China, the biggest rare-earth producer in the world, temporarily halted the export of its rare-earths to Japan. And headlines were again made in 2011 when China suspended rare earth production for one month in what some say was a bid to increase prices. Thankfully, metals don't just go up in smoke as oil does when it's used; they can be reclaimed from landfills and through recycling programs. However, years of waste, lack of tracking and the tiny percentage of materials that are reclaimable will make the process expensive and hazardous, thus adding to the price volatility of key metals. What I'm particularly worried about though is that so many people have pinned their hopes for future energy on cheaper, more efficient solar panels, without realising that the key materials used in current solar cells are also non-renewable. It's indicative of the thinking that there will always be another human invention or improvement to save us, so we don't actually need to curtail our use of and reliance on power, or the consumption of goods. Always believing that science and technology will save us means we don't actually feel any pressing need to simplify our lives or prepare our kids for a life of 'less'. Too many of us believe that there's always a 'solution' and that no sacrifices will need to be made.

Nuclear Incidents

We all know nuclear incidents and accidents aren't myths. Look at Hiroshima, Three Mile Island, Chernobyl, and now Fukushima. Look at the tonnes of yellowcake uranium found unguarded in the desert in Libya in September 2011. Look at the estimated 23,000 nuclear weapons in the world, a number the Federation of American Scientists says has actually dropped from a global high of 70,000 in 1986. Mmmm...makes me feel safer; now we can destroy the world a few thousand times less! The risks are probably even greater now because of the age of some of the nuclear power stations, the ideologies of various regimes, and the lack of safeguards in some countries where uranium hasn't been under as close a guard as it should have been. And hey, if someone really wants to cause large-scale destruction, radioactivity is a sure-fire way to get everybody sparked up! The old theory that the nuclear weapons arsenal would never be used (because of mutually assured destruction of the countries involved) was a sensibly misguided way of thinking in a time when the few players involved all followed the rules, but there are a lot of new kids on the block now, and some of them, frighteningly, aren't so concerned about the destruction part. Additionally, the push for "safe" nuclear energy doesn't take into account how all the radioactivity will be safely stored and disposed of 100 years from now when the world is undergoing oil stress and all the ramifications that go with it.

HEALTH ISSUES

Medical researchers have suggested that our children—yes, our kids, the ones we'll be tucking into bed tonight—will be the first Western kids in a century to have a shorter life span than their parents. That doesn't sound like the natural order of things, but you just need to look at all the processed food and fizzy drinks we fill ourselves with, the air we breathe, the stress we submit ourselves to, the time we spend sitting down and the chemicals that we come in contact with to understand why this is the medical profession's real fear. Add to that the effects of climate change spreading the natural habitat of mosquitoes, overuse of antibiotics and anti-bacterials that have led to new, drug-resistant strains of all kinds of diseases, and the rising incidence of health treatment—rather than prevention—and you can see why our children need all the help they can get in the health stakes. The disease of depression continues to incapacitate swathes of Westerners, and there probably aren't too many readers who don't know someone who has had their life cut short or been severely impacted by cancer, diabetes, heart disease, asthma or addiction. I know we all have to die sometime, but I don't want my kids (or myself) to gradually decay and eventually die from something that's entirely preventable. The strain on the public health system will be enormous as it struggles to cope with lingering, life-leeching, chronic diseases such as diabetes. There will be less able people in the workforce, and those healthy enough to work will be working harder and longer to pay for all the operating theatres, drugs and carers.

Nutrition

How is it possible that we can be overfed, yet undernourished? Obese, yet starving? The 1999–2000 Australian Diabetes, Obesity and Lifestyle Study indicated over seven million adult Australians aged 25 years and over (60%) were overweight. Of these, over two million (21%) were obese. In the US, the 2009 National Health & Nutrition Examination Survey found 12.5 million children aged 2–19 were obese. Our children are not only eating loads of sugar, salt, fat, processed foods and preservatives, but the healthy food they're eating is being shipped greater distances, sprayed with more chemicals, stored for longer and is most likely being grown in soils depleted of nutrients thanks to years of poor land management practice and the use of artificial fertilisers. Good health requires good nutrition, and you can't buy either in a packet.

Pandemics

SARS, bird flu, swine flu, and any yet-to-be-named, nasty, scientific-sounding superoozyfloozy diseases...if you believe that history repeats itself, then some time in the future, your child may experience a disease or virus that spreads rapidly through the community causing work, play, and day-to-day activities to grind to a halt, either temporarily or for a longer term and perhaps rendering many incapacitated or dead. The dangers of a pandemic are not just the disease and death it brings, but the shutting down of essential services when people either can't, aren't allowed to, or don't want to head in to work to keep the place ticking over. Imagine how you would cope if the electricity supply went down, or if food shops closed for a few weeks, or if there was no petrol being delivered to service stations because the refinery workers were all off sick. And don't forget to factor in the increased taxes we'll all be paying to cover the wonder drugs that are meant to grant us immunity.

Toxins

I remember reading about a cream that a doctor had prescribed for my daughter. I was happy to use it to fix her problem, but thought I'd do a bit of my own research. Thank God I did. I found a number of articles that had been published in reputable medical journals about this cream, and its link to an increase in a certain type of childhood cancer. Yes, the cream worked, but yes, for some children, it made them vulnerable to an even worse condition. How, I wondered, could this kind of cream get approval? How could it be so voraciously marketed to vulnerable parents? How could doctors prescribe it without mentioning the negative research findings? That's right, pharmaceuticals equals big business, that's how. Cosmetics, farming, manufacturing, energy and food are five key areas where toxins proliferate. In Rowan Jacobsen's book, *Fruitless Fall—the Collapse of the Honey Bee and the Coming Agricultural Crisis,* he probes the links between insecticides and how though one chemical may be deemed safe in isolation, when it comes in contact with another chemical in the environment the combination can become mind-blowingly toxic. Unfortunately, chemical companies aren't forced to test the results of their products in the real world!

Genetic engineering

Scientists have done a lot of good in this world, and an awful lot of bad. Genetic engineering of plants is pushed by corporations as the only way to feed the world, while the organic and heritage seed-saving networks feel incredibly fearful that it will impact normal plant species and the insects and animals that eat them. And what of the long-term effect of humans who eat genetically modified organisms (GMOs), or who eat animals that have been fed GMOs as their main ration? At first, it seems wonderful that a new strain of rice provides double or treble the previous yield, and/ or is resistant to some common problems, but when you realise that the seed cannot reproduce, and new supplies must be bought each year from a controlling corporation at an ever-higher price, you can see how the world's food supply is becoming increasingly controlled, and at risk. As I write, an Australian farmer, Steve Marsh, recently lost his organic certification status due to contamination of his crop by a neighbour's genetically modified crop. Where will it all end when these crops start to go wild, and where is the proof that GM foods are safe in the long term?

GLOBALISATION

Multinationals, global conglomerates, foreign governments and faceless investment funds are taking more and more control of the world's food supply, including the land itself, the seeds that are planted, the water, fertilisers and pesticides that are used, the supply chain, and the supermarkets where the products are eventually sold. Huge swathes of farming land continue to be snapped up by multinationals, and we all know that increasing concentration of vital resources in fewer hands can only mean that our food is going to get a lot more expensive, though not necessarily more nutritious! Currently in Australia and the United States, the insatiable appetite for domestic and export energy sees coal seam gas extraction receiving more rights than agriculture, pristine waterways or long-term residents—animal and human. One thing's for sure; you can't eat or drink gas.

Social Unrest

Social unrest is caused by a whole host of factors, including high unemployment, falling living standards, increased poverty, corruption, anti-immigrant sentiments, lack of community, lack of optimism and the widening gap between the rich and the poor. It can result in angry, violent protests against governments and corporations. Unless some big changes are made, we can expect to see a lot more social unrest in the years to come. The UK riots and the Occupy Wall Street movement gave us a sneak peek at this.

Terrorism

In John Pilger's book, *Freedom Next Time*, he writes: "On September 11, 2001, while the world lamented the deaths of 2,974 innocent people in the United States, the UN Food and Agricultural Organisation reported that another daily mortality rate continued: 36,615 children had died from the effects of extreme poverty." Whenever there is hardship and suffering in some part of the world, there will be bitterness, and extremists who seek redress any way they can. The terrorism genie can't be put back in the bottle without resolving inequity around the world, so unfortunately, terrorism, which wasn't even heard of a generation ago, has become normality rather than rarity. Bali, Mumbai, London, New York…we're still fighting and at the same time fuelling the beast.

The Squeezing of the Middle Class

There are a whole lot of people worse off than the middle class, but when middle class is all you know, and food prices keep going up, rates keep going up, insurance keeps going up, petrol keeps going up and education, health, compliance and insurance bills keep going up it's enough to bring anyone down! The 'working poor' sums up the squeeze being felt by many families as the ideals they grew up with of home ownership and just being able to pay their electricity bill become increasingly difficult. Meanwhile, multinational corporations and their shareholders rake in mega-profits, swooshing money around the world and into various projects and investments, making them even wealthier while scrupulously minimising the tax they pay at every step of the way. This further widens the gap between rich and poor, leaving the tax burden to the working class.

COMMUNICATIONS

Whenever we rely on something exclusively, we are at risk. Our personal computers and government and corporate computer systems are regularly hacked into and manipulated by criminal networks and foreign governments. In April 2011 the personal details of more than 77 million PlayStation users were easily hacked. Imagine the chaos if a bank's system was brought down for a week or an electricity grid mainframe was shut down. Having recently suffered electronic credit card fraud that twice drained our bank account, I realised how quickly and easily a family can be left high and dry by faceless fraudsters. Identity theft is also on the increase, and governments around the world are complaining about attacks on their electrical grids, nuclear systems, defence companies and banks. These are huge threats to the life we're used to leading.

The power, productivity, access to wisdom and connectivity that computers have given us are immense, but they have also increased our reliance on them, and therefore our vulnerability.

EVERYDAY HAZARDS

Unfortunately, in addition to all the future thinking we parents need to do, and suspenseful scenarios we need to ponder, we and our children face hazards that are far more in-your-face than nuclear missile launchers, hooded hackers and humanitarian crises. Our kids are facing showstoppers in their day-to-day lives caused solely by the nature of growing up in the Western world: nutritional deficiencies; alcohol abuse; drugs; obesity; eating disorders; bullying; peer-group pressure; school violence; early sex; STDs; unplanned pregnancy; dangerous driving; loneliness; social ineptness; self-mutilation; ADD; low self-esteem; depression; suicide. I often find myself laughing at the absurdity of trying to prepare kids for the really big-picture stuff while dealing with the day-to-day realities and hazards of bringing up kids 'Western'.

Advertising and Marketing

Advertising plays a huge role in our children's emotional, mental, physical and financial health. F. Scott Fitzgerald once said that "Advertising is a valuable economic factor because it is the cheapest way of selling goods, particularly if the goods are worthless." Our children are surrounded by marketing every day of their lives, and it's a critical factor in their overall wellbeing—or lack of—and that of the planet. Companies are now even paying not just for TV ads, bus sides and sports sponsorships, but for professional marketing direct to children inside their own classrooms. As the website of the UK's National Schools Partnership states: "At National Schools Partnership, we are the experts in using education to engage with children and families to achieve marketing results, learning impacts or social good. We reach and enthuse young people, parents and schools through formal and informal education routes in order to achieve a wide range of objectives for companies, brands, charities, trade organisations and public bodies."

So does that make our schools centres for learning or corporate profit centres for exploitation? Even taking the kids to an extra-curricular movie seemingly as benign as *The Smurfs* leaves a bad taste in the mouth when you realise how product placement so manipulates the young.

Instant Gratification

When we focus on instant gratification, we either deliberately or unconsciously blur our vision of the consequences of our actions. That's why we're now dealing with unprecedented levels of credit-card debt, high blood pressure, obesity and international high jinx. We're seduced by advertising and seek quick fixes: we're as likely to buy instant lottery tickets as we are to stick to a budget; we're as likely to call on a personal trainer or book in for liposuction as we are to change our eating habits; we're as likely to invade another country, be it militarily or economically, as we are to reduce our consumption, or innovate, or pay the true price of the limited resources we're consuming.

So yes, what with financial meltdowns, climate change, volatile oil prices, terrorism, natural disasters and tantrums...a lot can happen while we're checking out the snack bars in aisle three! But it's been my experience that by facing up to and acknowledging the fact that our children aren't living in a vaccum, but within a global context, we become free to explore and enjoy the many different areas that may help our children over the coming years.

For our family, that's meant everything from encouraging humour and self-awareness to questioning the status quo. It's meant we've focused on learning basic skills, spending more time in our community, widening our knowledge, setting ourselves challenges and producing in addition to consuming. It's been a lot of hard work and also a whole lot of fun.

Just as it takes many cells of honeycomb to make a honey bee colony resilient, it takes a childhood packed with love, adventure, learning and challenges to form a whole and capable adult who can walk tall into the future. The rest of this book is therefore devoted to offering up thoughts and practical ideas to help you empower your children to be able to cope with and contribute positively to the big issues of our time.

Part 2:
Raising Honeycomb Kids

··

*Life is either a daring adventure or nothing. To keep
our faces toward change and behave like free spirits
in the presence of fate is strength undefeatable.*

HELEN KELLER

*Tell me, I'll forget.
Show me, I may remember.
But involve me and I'll understand.*

CHINESE PROVERB

A successful beehive is a place of cooperation, industriousness, shared decision-making, planning, determination to survive together, reverence for nature, yummy stuff and a little bit of magic! Kind of like the ideal human family! So it doesn't matter if you came to this book out of fear for the future, out of incredible love for your children or grandchildren, or out of a deep compassion for humanity and the Earth as a whole; what matters is that by immersing yourself in ideas and actions that might make a difference, you become part of the solution, not a perpetuator of the problems. So, on to some ideas to get you buzzing!

Chapter 1

....

A SENSE OF COMMUNITY, CITIZENSHIP AND COOPERATION

Without a sense of caring, there can be no sense of community.

ANTHONY J. D'ANGELO

When all is said and done, the real citadel of strength of any community is in the hearts and minds and desires of those who dwell there.

EVERETT DIRKSEN

We make a living by what we get, but we make a life by what we give.

WINSTON CHURCHILL

Most of the hives I care for house bees who are gentle and hard to annoy, but there are two hives at the end of the row that house colonies that, more often than not, are bolshy and protective. At different times of the year and depending on the weather and the nectar they're eating, the bees can be inquisitive, calm, aggressive or nonchalant. Each individual beehive is a community with its own distinct personality, and funnily enough, I've found the same applies to car parks!

Small, wide-open or multi-storey, car parks are a fascinating microcosm of our communities. A few minutes in a car park and you tap into the relaxed mood of its citizens or feel their discontent!

How does your local car park rate? Do you feel yourself getting aggressive when you enter it? Do drivers barge past you or stay on your tail while you look for a spot? Have you seen cars duck into spots other people were lining up for? Do you hightail it past reversing drivers rather than stopping and letting them reverse unflustered? Do you lay on the horn and mutter under your breath while the kids cower in the backseat or worse, egg you on?

Kids these days learn a lot about life and our attitude to fellow citizens from the back seats of our cars. It's here they get to see what we do—not what we say to do. It's here they learn ways to react to disappointment and frustration. It's here they learn about courtesy and cooperation, or about selfishness and self-absorption. It's here they sense if we're happy and fulfilled, or tired and teed off. It's here they learn what we really think about community, and our role in it.

The difference in car-parking courtesy from my old suburban shopping centre to the one in the smaller community in which I now live is nothing short of amazing. I think there are a few reasons for this.

It's possible that in a large car park people feel they can be aggressive and rude because they don't expect to actually know you, i.e. they can get away with being rude because they're practically invisible among the thousands of other users. It's easy to be needlessly aggressive when you don't feel connected.

In a smaller town, you're much more aware and responsive to the idea that the other person trying to park their car may be a neighbour, or the parents of kids who go to school with your kids, or a tradesperson you deal with every now and then, and so you control yourself more and automatically show more consideration, and it's just the right thing to do really.

But whether there are 14 or 1,400 spots, we can easily decide to behave more politely and kindly next time we're in a car park. It's a choice. This is a special lesson for our children, as it teaches them to show care and respect not only for people they know, but also for those they don't. It teaches them that they're part of a community, and that a community needs respect, patience and cooperation if everyone is to find their place.

It's also possible that a larger car park signals a larger population centre, with its inherently more stressful lifestyle. It becomes easy for people with a self-centred view to imagine that they're the only ones who are stressed and in a rush; that they're the only ones with warring children on board; that they're the only ones who have to get a lot done in so little time. Perhaps a smaller town has a gentler pace of life, without so many pressures, or maybe the residents have other outlets for their stress, and let off the pressures in other ways and at more appropriate places than the local car park.

I have found both to be true. It was only a few weeks after moving from the city to a smaller community that I noticed a significant change in my driving habits. Gone was that stressful, finger-gripping hold on the steering wheel; after all, I had to use one hand to wave back at everybody who was waving at me!

In today's fast-paced world, it's much more natural for us to go out for a drink with our co-workers or collapse on the couch than to have a meaningful conversation or perform a selfless act for another citizen in our community. It's much easier for us to lay on our horn than lay off it. It's easier to cocoon ourselves inside than to emerge and reach out to those around us.

That's because many of us forge bonds well away from our homes due to the nature and location of our workplaces. And when we get home, we shut ourselves inside, trying to block out the annoying sounds of the stereo next door and the yapping dogs and the revving engines out in the street. Our home is our sanctuary, but it can also cut us off from a whole host of experiences and relationships that would make our lives, and those of our children, more fulfilling.

Think about the people living within a one-mile radius of you. How many of them do you really know? Do you know what they believe in? What makes them happy? What they do for a living? What they'd *really* like to do for a living? How many of them could you turn to for help? How many of them know what type of help you could offer? How many of them would you trust with your children? How many are happy? How many are suffering?

How do you teach your child that being independent and self-reliant has its advantages, but that being a part of a strong, healthy community is equally important? It's fairly easy. You just need to start getting out into it. Amongst it. Soon.

Jesper Juul, director of the Kempler Institute of Scandinavia and author of *Your Competent Child*, writes: "I firmly believe that having a sense of social responsibility enhances the quality of human life. We are all connected, for better or worse, and any notion that we can avoid influencing the lives of other people and being influenced by theirs is an illusion. The same principle applies to societies and families: there is no such thing as *your* problem and *my* problem. It is a question of *our* problem and *our* success."

'Community' is defined in the Oxford Dictionary as:

1. a group of people living in the same place or having a particular characteristic in common
2. the condition of sharing or having certain attitudes and interests in common
3. Ecology: a group of interdependent plants or animals growing or living together in natural conditions or occupying a specified habitat.

In Suzanne W. Morse's book, *Smart Communities*, she defines 'community' as the place where "individuals live, connect and are responsible for one another." Her opinion is that places that "develop strong identities for themselves while developing relationships with their neighbours hold the greatest promise for economic, social and civic success."

However you define 'community', however you try to ignore it, however you attempt to set yourself apart from it, it's likely that your children will need community more than you ever have… especially if oil price volatility continues and social unrest deepens.

Think about the type of community you want your child to live in. Is it different to the one you live in now? If so, how can you go about building the community you wish for?

The type of community I want for my kids is a safe, diverse, caring, self-reliant, fun and thriving one. It's one where attention is paid to community infrastructure, rather than just individual infrastructure. If we work at it, we can be part of this kind of community whether it's in the suburbs, the city or the country.

Whereas today a daily commute of two hours is seen as reasonable, in the future it simply may not be affordable or laudable. This voluntary or involuntary reining in of the commuter culture gives hope that a new importance will be placed on neighbours, local communities, local businesses and the local environment. One thing's for sure, 'local' is going to become more central to the lives of all citizens.

We're seeing this already in growing support for buying local and from farmers markets, and when people choose to buy from independent retailers rather than chain stores.

Have you ever suffered from cultural cringe? From thinking that the further away a product is made the better or more mysterious or more fashionable it is? That the further away from handmade or home-grown it is the better? I certainly have, but don't worry, it doesn't take much to reform—and it's incredibly rewarding!

Somehow, those wily marketers and transnationals convinced many of us that food and clothes and wine and furniture made overseas or interstate was better than anything we could grow or manufacture ourselves or buy from another local producer. We allowed them to hypnotise us into thinking that cheaper meant better; that the miles travelled equated to a journey worth taking; that support of local industries was the naive option for the unfashionable.

We've bought wine from interstate and overseas in preference to that made on farms three hours away. We've bought imported biscuits because they were cheaper than the locally made ones. We've ignored the op-shops, neighbourhood tailor and local designers for the big-name brands irresistibly peddled by celebrities. We've bought imported quilts, rather than the ones lovingly crafted by the lady down the road. But a return to shopping locally will help strengthen our community.

The people at the top end of the profit chain call this 'backward thinking' and 'protectionism', even 'activism', but there's nothing backward about wanting to support local businesses, the families who work in them and the communities they're part of and contribute to.

There are grassroots movements springing up all around the world encouraging people to think globally and act locally. People are being encouraged to eat local, seasonal foods, thus reducing environmental and health impacts that come from shipping foods halfway around the world.

Organised movements such as Transition Towns are all about relocalisation. Their desire is to prepare communities so that the bulk of their needs can be met locally. This means locally produced food, decreased energy reliance, local forms of energy creation and ownership, locally sourced building materials, local currency and even local waste management.

The philosophy is that by coming together, a community can enjoy a healthy economy, improved environmental conditions, a greater social bond and improved equality and opportunities, with the end goal being more purposeful and enjoyable lives. Hmm, sounds good to me!

At the heart of the Transition Towns movement is the philosophy that the rebuilding of community resilience and self-reliance is a way to face the increasing volatility of oil supplies and other perceived challenges.

There's probably already a transition town near you, from Totnes in England to Portobello in Scotland, Orewa in New Zealand, Bro Ddyfi in Wales, the Blue Mountains in Australia or Boulder in the USA. And if there isn't one near you, why not start your own?

That's the fun thing about communities, you can help shape them! You can nurture and encourage positive change, sustainable growth, youth engagement, important public resources and all sorts of enhancements and improvements. You just need to get involved.

After years of trying to be invisible in the suburbs, sticking to old friends and new workmates, I've recently discovered the joy of engaging with my local community. It's been so thoroughly enriching, I don't know why I never reached out from my little closed circle before. The excuse that I was 'too busy' was partly true, but I could have reduced my busyness to explore and accommodate my neighbours; I just never placed any importance on it. I didn't want to 'put myself out there' or 'intrude'. Even now, I'm very shy about meeting and engaging with people, but I sure understand why it's so important, and I've also now experienced how immensely rewarding it can be.

The people who have bubbled up in my local community are people our whole family now learns from, shares with, laughs with, trusts, relies upon and assists. Just the other week we attended a wonderful lunch held in our local community to celebrate Harmony Day. Everyone was invited to bring a dish that had something to do with their heritage. Seeing as we don't have a strong food tradition in our family, I just took something I liked to eat and was able to make with ingredients from the garden, a spicy Thai vegetable curry.

The local council donated the use of the hall for the get-together, we all brought our own cutlery, drinks and serving utensils, and wow—what a feast, what a celebration of locally grown food, what an array of food cooked with care and love. What an opportunity to sit down with people we'd never met before, as well as to hang out with those we wanted to get to know better.

The mood was relaxed and jovial, the food delicious and diverse. It was a great way to truly feel part of the community and to contribute to it...and we had leftovers and laughs for days!

Isn't it exciting to think that in your children's future there might be an enthusiastic return to such old-fashioned values of community and citizenship?

Encourage your children to connect and be connected, and they'll experience all the pleasure and support that comes with that.

By reaching out to your community, you'll be teaching your children to learn how to get along with others, how to listen and to be listened to, how to contribute, how to receive, and how to support and be supported.

Yet another benefit is the general peace of mind that comes from knowing that you can turn to more than one neighbour for help—as well as offer it. This means that if you ever need it, help will arrive a whole lot sooner than if you're left waiting for the authorities to turn up. You'll also be able to band together against any threats, organise resources as needed, help set an upbeat, resourceful tone for your area and discover all sorts of opportunities.

As a member of a community, you have a wider role to play than the one that you play in your own family. It's time to entertain the thought that you could be a role model to children other than your own. You and your children don't live in isolation, so if you can have a positive impact on the children who will be your children's peers, that can benefit not only the children in question, but your own children as well.

It's up to us to lead by example and help our children pick up the rubbish at the skateboard park. It's up to us to take a dish to a neighbour who we know would appreciate a home-cooked meal. It's up to us to be welcoming when a new person moves in, rather than waiting for them to visit us because we feel 'too shy'. It's up to us to act warmly and with care, not necessarily sternly, when we see unaccompanied children doing things they shouldn't.

In some ways, we in the West have been allowed to become quite superficial because truly intimate relationships with our local community have broken down. We tend to judge people at face value because that's all we know about them. However, when relationships are strong and community ties are cherished, we know the reality of who our neighbours are and what's really going on in their lives, because we've seen them grow up, we know people who went to school with them, we've worked with them, we've been there for their achievements and losses, we've been to the funerals of their loved ones. Once I might have found this suffocating because I quite like anonymity, but knowing that everyone has ups and downs creates real relationships, and there's less pressure to be perfect. The highs are celebrated, and the lows aren't hidden away.

Some of us might feel like we don't have a connection to the area we live in. Perhaps we plan to move out soon. Perhaps we're just in a town because of a work posting. Perhaps we just can't be bothered engaging. But it's crucial that our children discover their role in the community, and how they can learn from, grow with, contribute to and benefit from it. Introduce them around so they get known; it's the only way for people to realise they're individuals with unique personalities and gifts to offer, rather than just strangers and pests.

The African proverb "It takes a village to raise a child" is as true in the West as it is in the East. My heart has been so warmed by the number of lovely people in our community who go out of their way to make our children feel welcome at events, even though the events are really aimed at the adults (many of them retired or without children). By reaching out to children and making them feel welcome, these people are helping to build our diverse community from the bottom up. They're showing that they're true community builders, not gated community escapees. That's not to say that children should be allowed to run riot, but by allowing them to contribute and feel welcome in their community means that they'll grow up feeling respected, and be more inclined to act respectfully!

As a teenager, I was in a charity group that visited old people's homes and helped out street kids. My parents encouraged me to join the group, and I did it because it was fun to be out with my friends, not because I was a saint. Peers were also the reason I was a volunteer lifeguard for many years. I wasn't really driven by a desire to save people's lives in the surf, but by being able to be out and about and independent, without my parents looking over my shoulder all the time.

Both these stints doing community work, even though my initial reasons were shallow, left a lasting impression on me. I realised how lonely and poorly treated old people could be. I saw teens my own age without a safety net. I was able to use the first aid skills I'd learned as a lifeguard to help road accident victims years later. I also learned that it feels good to help, not in a skin-deep kind of way, but deep in one's soul for years to come.

When I was seventeen and living in America on a youth exchange program, I received a call from a friend of mine who wanted to surprise his aunty by painting the outside of her decrepit house while she was at work. It sounded like fun, so I was in. We toiled the whole day, turning the greyest, ugliest, most ramshackle house in the street into the prettiest. We nailed up gutters, sanded, and then painted the front a creamy yellow with fun aqua-blue gutters, window frames and details. It was hard work, but it was happy work. The neighbours driving by honked their horns and gave us the thumbs up. When she arrived home, my friend's aunty collapsed in tears when she saw our admittedly amateurish handiwork. At first I thought she hated it, but it soon became clear that it wasn't the paint job she was crying about; it was the overwhelming feeling of connection and love.

I recount this story because many parents don't think their kids are capable of painting a house, or working unsupervised, or helping out. Well, if we don't give them the opportunity, we—and they—will never know. Kids can have fun while helping others in the community, and they'll also receive a sensational boost to their self-esteem and sense of worth.

I just turned to my son and asked him what he thought 'community' was. He said, "Community is about saving the world," and then he did an enormous burp and smiled! Ah, the wisdom and ways of kids.

In John Pilger's book, *Freedom Next Time*, he writes, "Ubunti is a subtle concept from the Nguni languages (South Africa) that says a person's humanity is expressed through empathy and solidarity with others: through community and standing together. A Xhosa proverb is 'Ubuntu ungamntu ngabanye abantu'—'People are people through other people.'"

What a great understanding of the link between the individual and community. Perhaps it's time we strengthened our own links. When you reach out, it won't only be your child who'll benefit, everyone will.

THOUGHT LAUNCHERS & CONVERSATION STARTERS

- Think about and write down **what you and your family are for**, rather than what you're against...then stick it on the fridge or the toilet door!
- **Ask the kids what they like best** about your local community.
- Ask yourself what **areas of concern** you have for your community (vandalism, youth boredom, fast pace, lack of meaningful communication, lack of control of vital resources, pollution, not enough employment opportunities close to

home, too much noise, high school drop-out rate, general lack of connection, etc.).

- Find out about some of the **local-interest groups** operating in the area, from sports clubs to knitting groups, landcare groups to seed-savers and gardeners, scouts to church groups. Which ones might you and your children like to try?
- Find out about some of the **'at need' groups** in your community. Is there a way you and your kids can offer help (e.g., taking your family pet to visit old people at a nursing home, or tidying up a garden for a busy neighbour, or fetching groceries for a new mum, or organising a get-together for people who have moved to the area).
- Is there some kind of **community event** you could establish such as a once-a-month swap day, or a farmers/growers market, or craft sale?
- Is there an **area in your community you can adopt** and keep free of litter and well maintained? A corner of a local park? The walkway to the shops? The treed area by the side of the road?
- Work with your **local council** to attract socially and environmentally responsible industries to your area to help secure more local jobs.
- If it's your children's peers who will end up influencing them, have you ever thought of **sponsoring a disadvantaged child** in your community to attend pre-school for a couple of days a week? This would offer a child a chance, in those crucial early years, to experience a different type of childraising that he or she might not have experienced at home, thus helping them to adapt better to school and get a better start than they otherwise would have.
- What tools and implements could you **share with or lend** to your neighbours?
- Have you heard about a development in your area that you have misgivings about? Show your child that it's important

to have a voice. Organise a **creative and fun protest** to draw attention to the matter.

- Think about **'giving loops'** you can create, like making extra serves of a meal so your neighbours can have a night off cooking while you get a night off the following week when they reciprocate. Perhaps you mow your own and your neighbours' lawns this month, and they reciprocate next month. What other 'giving loops' can you think of that would benefit you and other people in your community so as to show your kids the benefits of cooperation?

- **Volunteer** to help a charity that is helping immigrants to settle into your country, and take the whole family along. Make friends, not enemies, by helping to smooth their way and by making them feel welcome. Be a patient companion as they learn to integrate into the community.

- Join or set up a **'time bank'** in your community where you trade an hour of your work for an hour of someone else's skills. Everyone's hour has the same value, so you might trade an hour of gardening or house cleaning for an hour of professional photography or legal services. You might trade an hour of driving an elderly person to appointments or the shops for an hour's foreign language tuition for your children, or for a musician to perform at a party. The more people who join a local time bank, the wider the variety of services you can access and choose from. You can even set up a time bank within your own family, so the kids can swap say an hour of chore time, for an hour of playing games with you! For more about time banks, visit www.timebanks.org.

- Investigate what local groups members of your family could join as **volunteers** so you can offer help when it's needed, as well as learning valuable skills, e.g. St John Ambulance, the local fire brigade, volunteer lifeguards, etc.

- Buy a book on **first aid** so you have information handy if you need it, and book in for a first aid course.

- **Join a local emergency services crew,** volunteer fire brigade or first-responders team so you're able to assist other local citizens and learn valuable skills in the process. This will help teach your children the importance of community action. You'll also be able to pass on the skills you've learned to your kids, and it's a great way to meet people in your local area.
- Think deeply about what kind of shared community facilities and services might be of benefit to your town in the future. Shared transport? Specific community buildings with facilities all can use? Water? Energy? And see what you can get started.

Chapter 2

SMART THINKING

*By three methods we may learn wisdom: first, by reflection,
which is noblest; second, by imitation, which is easiest;
and third by experience, which is the bitterest.*

Confucius

*Perhaps no place in any community is so totally democratic as
the town library. The only entrance requirement is interest.*

Lady Bird Johnson

No problem can stand the assault of sustained thinking.

Voltaire

Keep your eyes and ears open and you may notice that there aren't that many people thinking for themselves anymore. It seems that more and more, we're relying on the views and choices of newscasters, talkback radio, print media, reality TV, advertisers and corporations rather than arriving at our own positions. It starts young.

Back in 1990, New York teacher-of-the-year John Taylor Gatto, in his acceptance speech, said:

Two institutions at present control our children's lives—television and schooling, in that order. Both of these reduce the real world of wisdom, fortitude, temperance, and justice to a never-ending, non-stopping abstraction. In centuries past the time of a child and adolescent would be occupied in real work, real charity, real adventures, and the realistic search for mentors who might teach what you really wanted to learn. A great deal of time was spent in community pursuits, practicing affection, meeting and studying every level of the community, learning how to make a home, and dozens of other tasks necessary to become a whole man or woman.

John Taylor Gatto believes that children no longer have the free hours they need to truly learn and develop; that they spend their time watching people on TV pretending to be real people, rather than actually interacting with real people; that they spend their time in school learning how to become unquestioning adult workers for life.

Compulsory testing in our school systems means that our children are being coached to pass exams, rather than being encouraged to reason, analyse, problem solve, critique, brainstorm, weigh things up, create and philosophise.

Think about it...schools teach our kids to obey, but do they teach them to think? Schools teach our kids to stop what they're working on when they hear a bell, but do they encourage them to extend their passion? And what of the fact that schools are, for the most part, set up to prepare our children to enter into careers rather than callings.

In many ways, due to everything from budget restrictions to entrenched views and government directives, schools tend to be teaching ignorance alongside insight, and conformity to the detriment of creativity. There are lots of great teachers out there of course, but increasing numbers of families are starting to explore alternative-type schools such as Montessori and Steiner, along with home-based natural learning for just these reasons.

If you want your children to be curious, to be up for a challenge, to be creative problem solvers and to be able to teach themselves, not simply be taught, then you have to invest more than just school fees in their education.

Encouraging our kids to think is important because when our children aren't taught to think, it's much easier for them to be swayed by uninformed peer groups and adults, and to be sold products they don't need. Their view of the world will be like that of a horse wearing blinkers. They'll think they have choices and opinions, but in reality, their choices and opinions will be those espoused by the people, companies and governments with the biggest budgets, the highest pulpits, the most potent power, the most razzle dazzle.

Another area of institutional schooling that doesn't work for every child is the narrow definition of 'intelligence' as measured by the academic world. For example, a friend of mine has two children, one a natural academic, the other a natural woodworker. It breaks her heart to see her 'carpenter' treated as a failure in the school system, even though his talent will remain a valuable one in the years ahead. Unfortunately, it's hard to build a healthy self-esteem when your report card keeps telling you you're a failure.

According to Professor Howard Gardner, author of *Multiple Intelligences* and *Intelligence Reframed*, we all have some type of intelligence (Mathematical-Logical, Bodily-Kinesthetic, Musical, Inter-personal, Intra-personal, Linguistic, Spatial and/or Naturalistic), so as parents, we need to find out HOW our children are intelligent, and then champion that intelligence. It might be that they are good with people, have high stamina, have a way with animals, think logically, or have the gift of music. We all have gifts, it's just that some are overrated and some are underrated, depending on the society in which we live.

A sad disservice is also often paid to high-IQ kids when they're pushed towards careers that don't satisfy their soul, e.g. doctors with no bedside manner, lawyers who wanted to be teachers, engineers who wanted to be artists. That's because kids who get high marks often aren't allowed to follow their passions; instead, they're forced to choose from a prescribed list of high-score careers. They can also struggle as they come to discover that being successful in school doesn't automatically mean that they're successful in the workplace, where emotional intelligence and self-discipline come into play.

Start noticing what your children are naturally drawn to: is it art? Animals? Movement? Arithmetic? People? This is not necessarily what they're good at, but what they're absorbed by. Absorption is the key, because when our children experience this, it's called being 'in the zone', or 'in the flow'.

Bees experience 'flow' too. It's called a 'honey flow'. This is when the conditions are perfect, the sun is out, the wind is calm and the trees are flowering, churning out nectar and pollen. When a honey flow is on, the bees take to the skies, caught in the moment, naturally capitalising on the abundance of life, and doing what they do best.

I'm good at hanging out clothes (though my husband might disagree!), scheduling meetings and writing website code, but I don't particularly enjoy doing those things. It's when I'm digging in the garden, beekeeping, taking photographs, discovering something new, caring for animals or writing that I get lost in the moment. That's my 'zone', and time spent doing these things brings me great contentment. The more of that we can have in our lives, the better!

The broader our horizons, the more likely we are to stumble upon what makes us feel whole. That's why helping to develop our children's love of and respect for reading has to be one of the most valuable gifts we can give our children. It's through books (if they read authors of different styles and opinions) that they can experience marvels and mystery, triumph and tears, and far-away and special spaces. They can learn about fact and fiction, philosophy and finality, and about any subject they ever show an interest in.

Books are so valuable to the wisdom and wellbeing of societies, to culture, to hearts, to minds, to morale, to self-reliance, to self-respect, to history and to the imagination that since the earliest of days brutal regimes have ordered the ceremonial destruction and burning of them. Books help to broaden our ideas, introduce us to characters we don't find in our own families, and help us to anticipate potential scenarios and solutions, as well as giving us concrete advice and instruction.

Books also enable our children to walk a mile in the shoes of millions of different people living very different lives. They help us all to turn over a new leaf, and help to build empathy.

Our family bookcase is full of whimsical texts, page-turners, botanical guides and 'how-to' manuals. Our kids have never shown much interest in the potboilers and bestsellers on the shelves, but wow, they pore over the books on health and healing, animal care, gardening and bugs. We first realised this when our then seven-year-old daughter started giving us first aid tips and assuring us that she could now deliver a baby because she'd read a book called *Where There is No Doctor*. My initial reaction was that she was too young to see line drawings of genitals and broken limbs, wounds and pustules, and that we'd have to put G, M & R ratings on the shelves, but she was completely unfazed, because she'd discovered true knowledge, not mere titillation. Last time I cut myself in the garden, she ran to the mulberry tree, stripped a leaf, and wound it around my finger. "I read it in the book, Mum. That's how you stop the bleeding," she said proudly.

Your children's future will be so much brighter if they have access to and an appreciation for books. And if you make literacy a goal, not just for your own children, but for children in your neighbourhood and around the world, the lives of everyone will be improved.

Our children will also benefit if we encourage them to think, not just to learn. Mastering thinking is more important than mastering a specific technology that could well be outdated by the time they finish their studies. By learning to think, they'll be able to find the answers to many difficult questions, and to help others as well.

It's easy to introduce the skill of thinking to our children, to teach them that there can be many answers to a question, many reasons for a result. It can be as simple as asking a question when a car overtakes yours: "Why do you think that driver is in such a hurry that he feels the need to break the speed limit?" Their answers could be as diverse as:

Because he slept in and is late for work

Because it's an emergency, his wife is sick in hospital

Because his boss will give him the sack if he's late

Because he's not feeling happy with himself today

Because he feels powerful when he's driving

Because he's a racing-car driver.

The next step is to ask your children for their thoughts on solving some of these problems the driver might have. "What are some solutions the driver could implement so that he doesn't need to speed?" Again, the answers will be diverse:

Get a wind-up alarm clock so that when the power goes out, his clock will still work

Call the police to give him a safe escort to see his sick wife, and if they can't come, he should put on his emergency lights so people know something is wrong

He should get up earlier so he's not late, or he should find a more understanding boss

He needs to find some hobbies and some good friends and do some good deeds so he doesn't feel so grumpy

He needs to work out that being in control of your life makes you feel much better than being in control of a car

He needs to learn to only go fast on the racetrack, not on a regular road!

Ask your children to think about their own behaviours and actions. Ask them to think about other ways they could have handled themselves, or the different ways they might react to a problem. Help them to develop self-knowledge; it's the best self-help there is!

For example, many of us believe that the way we think is unchangeable. Teaching kids that there are all kinds of different reactions they could have to the same problem means that there will never be an event in their life that is totally beyond their control. For example, if they lose a game of soccer they can think they're hopeless, think their team needs more training, blame the weather, congratulate the other team and use them as inspiration, rationalise that not many people win every time, or shift their focus away from the outcome to how much fun it was to run around in the rain. When our children are aware of how they think, and of how they can change the way they think, no event will ever have the power to completely derail their lives.

Don't always jump in to solve a problem for them, either. Encourage them to find solutions of their own, and be there to help guide them along the way. The more problem solving they experience, the greater the gaining of wisdom. On that note—it's not about answering for them either. Let them think about their own answer to a question directed to them, however much you want to butt in.

Wisdom is about knowing that you don't have all the answers, but being open to finding them, and being active in their pursuit. It's about being flexible, insightful and broad-minded. A wise person doesn't fly off the handle; a wise person calmly contemplates, arriving at the best possible decision, while being open to making an even better one given new information or circumstances.

Wisdom also involves gut reaction, intuition and insight. Teach your children to trust themselves. If something feels or looks wrong, it probably is. If they don't trust someone, there's probably a good reason. Encourage your children to take time to think about the things that make them uncomfortable, rather than trying to ignore the voice in their head. This awareness could save or enhance their life. Instinct is key.

The whole area of philosophy is one from which we can all benefit immensely. The writings of Aristotle, Augustine, Emerson, Gandhi, Gibran, the Dalai Lama, Plato, Thoreau, Lao Tzu and many others allow you to gain from years of learning while building your own personal philosophy of life. That's the amazing thing about life now; we don't need to start from scratch. We can choose the best of the best while adding our own special ingredients to our views and the living of our lives. By sharing a variety of philosophies with our children, we'll give them a great opportunity to make sense of the events and people around them, and to come up with well-thought-out solutions.

As British philosopher Bertrand Russell once said, "The good life is one inspired by love and guided by knowledge."

THOUGHT LAUNCHERS & CONVERSATION STARTERS

- Encourage your children to **make up theories** as to why things happen. Don't correct them if they're wrong, but if you know the real reason, introduce it into the conversation, along with some other possibilities.
- Play lots of **'what if'** games, e.g., "How could we get to Nanna's if we didn't have a car?" "How could we keep the grass down if we couldn't run our lawnmower?" "How much might food cost if the farmers had to pay lots more to fill their tractors?"
- How many times each week do your children see you read? The best way to teach your children the importance

of **reading** is to let them see your own commitment to and enjoyment of it.

- Help with reading at a local school, or support a charity that supplies **books to disadvantaged people** in your country and overseas.
- Draw up a chart so your children can see how many minutes/hours each week are devoted to various activities. Ask them to track what they do with their **leisure time** so they can see where their time is spent. Is reading a book well up the list, or is it eclipsed by time spent watching TV or playing computer games?
- Ask your children what their favourite book series is. If they haven't read them all, encourage them to **ask the librarian** to see if they can get more of the series in.
- If your children don't know what to get you for a birthday present, ask them to **write you a mini-book**.
- Next time your children ask you a question, **encourage them to think** about possible answers, and once they've had a crack at it, point them to books where other answers may be found.
- Play **word games** with your kids to extend their vocabulary, e.g. ask them to name a similar word to one you give them, or ask them to make one up!
- For fun, come up with a **family slogan** using made-up words that only your family understands.
- Whenever the opportunity presents, ask your children to come up with **three different reasons** to explain an event or action that they witness.
- Take your children to **open days** at various churches and cultural institutions. Host open days of your own, and invite people from other cultures and backgrounds to yours so you can be exposed to different ideas.
- Don't just invite kids or adults to your home who are of the same ethnic or **socio-demographic group** as yours;

open your reach wider to explore that all-important bigger picture.

- Borrow some books on **philosophy** from the library, and learn more about some of the great thinkers.

Chapter 3

BUILDING HOPE AND RESILIENCE

*Hope is definitely not the same thing as optimism. It is not the
conviction that something will turn out well, but the certainty
that something makes sense, regardless of how it turns out.*

VACLAV HAVEL

*Resilience—the capacity of a system to absorb disturbance and
reorganise while undergoing change, so as to retain essentially
the same function, structure, identity and feedbacks.*

ROB HOPKINS

*In order to succeed, people need a sense of self-
efficacy, to struggle together with resilience to meet
the inevitable obstacles and inequities of life.*

ALBERT BANDURA

To have belief that through your actions, you can
reach certain goals and produce certain effects; that's
what 'self-efficacy' means. After reading about all the problems we

face, you might feel like the most effective thing you can do is take a headache tablet and have a good lie down. Don't despair! Don't lose sight of the big picture. Just because the future may not be all shiny shopping malls, it doesn't mean it won't be a whole lot of fun, along with being inspiring, interesting, exciting, exhilarating and fulfilling for your children (and for you, too!).

Being hopeful is about perception. It's about giving your children the chance to face challenges head-on and to make sure the little voice inside their head speaks more sunshine than gloom. What's that old saying? Every cloud has a silver lining. Well, it's only true if you go looking for it. As Abraham Lincoln said, "Most people are as happy as they make up their mind to be."

So, how do you bring up your children to see the rainbows on rainy days? How do you encourage them to be realistically optimistic while at the same time building their resilience so they're able to face all the curve balls of the future? How do you nurture their belief in themselves so they have the ability to shape, affect and respond to a variety of outcomes?

You can begin by providing them with lots of small challenges, ones they can successfully master. Psychologists believe that this develops their self-esteem in a healthy way, as opposed to just inflating it.

Children who are set challenges way above their level of expertise, or who are forced to compete in a skill area for which they are not adequately equipped, suffer as a consequence. As do children whose parents do everything for them or who are constantly told their work is great, even when it's not. When everything they do receives the same amount of praise, kids find it hard to tell what genuine praise really is. It becomes difficult for them to distinguish what's good, what's so-so and what really needs improvement.

Think about it: is every piece of artwork your child does really fabulous? Is your child really the best player on the team in every game? We need to encourage and love our kids, and give them a soft place to fall when they fail. We need to avoid badgering, belittling and bemoaning their efforts and skills. But we also need to avoid overdoing the praise when it's not warranted, as this takes away their ability to master and judge themselves.

If our children are always judged they can't just enjoy. If our children are told they're doing well, regardless of how they do, they have no incentive to become better, learn more, or stretch themselves. For example, our daughter loves horse riding. If she doesn't know there's room for improvement, she'll never discover that the best way to improve her horse management skills is by training regularly, asking experts for tips, building up her strength, improving her fitness and studying real masters of the ring. By not circumventing this exploration with false praise, she learns that there are many elements to success, a key one of which is 'effort'. She also learns that goals can only be reached by working toward them bit by bit. Funnily enough, this is what the real world of not-so-unconditional love also requires!

In Martin P. Seligman's book, *The Optimistic Child*, he suggests that you need to give your children the opportunity to achieve many small things so they can feel success. The more they try and succeed, the more positive they'll feel about themselves, and the more persistent they'll become when things go wrong.

Seligman's wonderful book contains plenty of information about how to develop your child's self-esteem in a healthy way. Many of his findings ring true for me, especially his commentary about the potential for "psychological immunisation".

My mum had polio as a child. She was in a convalescent home for much of her childhood, and has been crippled all her life. Having had first-hand experience of the devastating effects of polio, she had us all vaccinated at an early age, knowing that minuscule doses of the virus, administered a number of times, built immunity. The field of vaccination is now mired in controversy, but it's the idea behind it that's so interesting. Perhaps, as Seligman suggested, you may be able to 'mentally vaccinate' your children through small successes, thus preparing them for a mentally healthy future.

We're trying to apply his advice with our children, in small doses, from letting them cook simple meals to encouraging them to go off fishing on their own. We give them small doses of skills training, like giving them a real tool kit and some wood, and seeing what they do with it. We give them small doses of age-appropriate challenging scenarios—like working out how to hang clothes on a line that they can't reach, turning food on a BBQ without getting burnt, vacuuming the car, and preparing their own garden beds.

We encourage them to climb trees, bang in nails, find caterpillars, take their plates to the kitchen, juice their own oranges, sort their laundry, cook dinner and take flashlights out to explore the dark in the hope that lots of small successes when they are young will enable them to take on even bigger challenges as they grow up.

When kids truly achieve and accomplish things, their self-esteem builds naturally. By giving our children small doses of all sorts of things—the mundane and the magical—we hope they'll be ready to face their future with a healthy attitude and a realistically positive frame of mind.

Your frame of mind is really important too. For many of us who have experienced luxuries unknown to previous generations, coming to terms with a possible reduction in choice and living standards can be really confronting, so much so that initially your reaction may be, "I wouldn't want to live in a world like that if I couldn't afford to go to a restaurant/I was that sick/there was intermittent power/coffee was unaffordable/I couldn't drive as much/there was war"...name your fear.

However, when my beautiful Aunty Mary was dying of cancer, my Uncle John said to me: "All these people who say they wouldn't want to live to be ninety-nine, well I'll tell you something, anyone who is ninety-eight wants to live to be ninety-nine!"

He summed up so beautifully the overwhelming will of people to live; to be alive; to stay. And so, in your own and your children's future, life will still be worth living, even if it isn't as cushy and predictable and unrestricted as it is now...but who knows? I'm optimistic that on a deeper scale—not the superficial one many of us have come to measure ourselves by—life may well be a whole lot more fulfilling.

So, with life as our choice, our aim is for our kids to be hopeful, not fearful. We want them to be able to approach any challenge that comes their way in an upfront, confident, give-it-a-go manner.

When our children are faced with difficulties in life, wouldn't it be great for them if they didn't just throw their hands up in the air and wait to be rescued, but instead, draw—after their initial shock, discomfort and disappointment—on their internal courage to start working confidently, competently and contentedly on a solution. That's resilience, the ability to be able to come back from disappointment rather than plummeting into despair.

They'll have a better chance of being resilient if they're self-directed. Self-direction is about being able to look inward for comfort and confidence, rather than outward. It's about being able to acknowledge their own strengths and weaknesses, rather than having to look to you (or their boss or their peers) for approval or disapproval.

And you can help. Instead of saying, "You played great," you might ask them, "How did that game feel?" If they start slamming themselves, saying they played terribly, you might acknowledge that it wasn't their best game, but you could also help them to see that it wasn't all bad by saying, "True, but how did you feel when you got that shot from the corner?" In other words, ask them how *they* think they did, rather than tell them how *you* think they did! If they think they did—and they did do—poorly, ask them about their ideas as to how they could improve or approach it differently next time before you offer your own constructive advice.

Self-reliance is another key factor in how your children will fare as adults. Self-reliance doesn't mean taking care of oneself at the expense of others; it simply means that your children won't have to be dependent on welfare, on the government, on corporations, or on systems. If they're self-directed, it also means they won't need to be reliant on other people's attitudes either; it will mean they're capable. It will mean they're able to contribute. All this will feed into their self-esteem and optimism.

Resilience and self-reliance bring an end to the blame game. First and foremost, you accept responsibility for yourself. Sure, it's great if someone, or a group, or a government steps in to help you out, but you shouldn't put all your eggs in one basket and become reliant on them. After all, look what happened to the people of New Orleans, who were as ill-prepared for Hurricane Katrina as the rescue effort.

It's like bees, they don't wait around for a courier delivery of honey from the drone squad; they're out there every day finding nectar, bagging up pollen, and collecting tree resin to make propolis that they use to keep the hive healthy. They know it's up to them to plan and prepare, to stock up and reduce their reliance on the fickle flowers of winter.

I know that confidence in my own ability to look after myself and my family lessens my anxiety and gives me great contentment. We're no longer totally dependent on fuel-filled trucks to bring food to the mall to feed us. We've learned the basics of self-sufficiency and first aid, we've tried to minimise our debt, and we've thought about what trees will be needed on our property 30, 50, 150 years down the track. But how do we help our children move toward this mark? How do we instil hope into our children?

These days, we're more likely to shield our children, wrapping them in cotton wool, rather than exposing them to the small challenges they must face in order to grow up. Child psychologist Dr John Irvine lamented that these days even playgrounds have become so safe that they offer children limited challenges to test their skills and grow as people. Whereas once we were allowed to walk down the street and hang out in the park, now we keep our kids behind locked doors and gates.

We need to find a balance between protecting our kids and carefully and gently exposing them to challenges and perceived danger.

A robust child has the best chance of becoming a robust adult, but if we never allow our children to develop that robustness, what kind of adults will they become?

Anyone who's ever been thrown by a horse knows they need to 'get back in the saddle'. This wonderful saying helps focus on the need to get past setbacks, to be persistent, to not give up, or give in to your fears. To build courage and competence.

One way to get past everyday setbacks is to understand, yet not overplay the problem. Another is to avoid using catastrophic language (always, never, the worst, etc.), and to think about possible solutions, or ways to make the most of the problem.

These are all things that can help lead to a satisfying, happy life, complete with meaning, purpose and optimism.

By empowering our children rather than inflating them, we encourage them to be comfortable within their own skin. By giving them small challenges they can confront successfully, we give them the internal fortitude to be able to face more significant challenges later on. By exhibiting optimism, we encourage its embodiment.

As the Mental Health Foundation of Australia says, "Resilience is about always being tougher than your life is." I reckon that sums it up perfectly.

THOUGHT LAUNCHERS & CONVERSATION STARTERS

- Ask your children to think up some ways in which they'd enjoy **contributing to the household** (rather than you choosing the chores for them).
- When something bad happens, ask them if they can see any **positives** from what has occurred (if they can't, help them by suggesting some ideas).

- After a sports game or artistic performance, invite them to give themselves **their own feedback** before you join in.
- Invite them to write a **letter to the editor** of your local newspaper regarding an issue they're concerned about, so that they can feel that their voice is being heard.
- Pop a note on the kitchen fridge **listing words** that can replace 'catastrophic' ones, e.g. 'a long time' instead of 'never', 'sometimes' instead of 'always', 'some people' instead of 'everyone', etc.
- Ask them what they were proud of achieving today, and tell them about the **small challenge**s you also overcame during the course of the day.
- Ask your children to come up with some **descriptive words** (eg: kind, sporty, funny) that they'd like to be associated with them. Ask them to think of things they could do to align their actions with those words.
- Think about the importance of language, and **modify** how you say things, e.g., instead of saying "I'll stand here in case you fall," which might make a child feel that you don't think they're capable, say "I'll stand here in case you feel a little wobbly."
- Ask them what their **proudest moments** are, what has given them the greatest sense of satisfaction.
- Once a week, have them set themselves a **small mission.** It might be to make a grumpy teacher smile, to be nice to a younger kid, or to say no when they're asked to do something that they know isn't right. Then, at the end of the week, congratulate them on achieving their goal, or help them work out why they didn't.

Think of some challenges around the house and further afield that you can give your children so that they can experience lots of small successes. For example, have them:

- **Climb** a ladder to the top rung
- **Clean** the bathtub all by themselves
- Go on a **scavenger hunt** around your local park
- **Care** for a younger child or elderly relative for a set time
- **Identify** and bring you items from the kitchen drawer or your tool kit
- **Make their own** sandwiches for school, or make lunch for the whole family on the weekend
- **Do** the grocery shopping: supply them with a list and money and be nearby to help if needed.
- Book in for a **first aid course** with your children, and learn alongside them the basic and vital skills needed to render aid and save lives.

And add more challenges of your own!

Chapter 4

COMPETITION VS CONNECTION

Competition has been shown to be useful up to a certain point and no further, but cooperation, which is the thing we must strive for today, begins where competition leaves off.

FRANKLIN D. ROOSEVELT

The only thing that will redeem mankind is cooperation.

BERTRAND RUSSELL

We live in a world where there are billions more losers than winners, so our children will benefit many times over from the lessons you can teach them now about cooperation versus competition. A great place to start is at a beehive. At a beehive you will see bees cooperating to create a remarkably successful society, but to see the alternative, watch two political parties go head to head or get an invite to a child's birthday party and see what you can observe!

Have you ever watched your children play musical chairs? Have you ever seen it descend into chaos, tears and tantrums? I have. It was at our daughter's birthday party. She was turning four, and we did what a zillion other parents before us have done. We played that timeless favourite, musical chairs.

Lots of harmless fun you'd think. Then we noticed that the kids had started pushing each other, skulking around and tripping each other up, in short, cheating and scheming. It made me wonder if there was a SWAT team for preschoolers as it looked like we might need to break the party up! The kids weren't in any way learning how to play together nicely. We'd actually taught them that getting to the chair was more important than their care of others, a message that wasn't in the spirit of the party, or in anyone's best interests.

I remember feeling uneasy, disquieted, but I pushed it to the back of my mind for years, until one day I came across Canadian man Jim Deacove. Jim runs a company called Family Pastimes. He's a board-game maker, but one with a difference. All of his games are aimed at bringing out cooperation, rather than competition. His belief is that people should play the game, not each other.

He has a wonderful take on musical chairs. The cooperative way to play it is to still take a chair away each time the music stops, but instead of fighting over the remaining chairs, the kids have to cooperate to try and fit everyone on the remaining ones. Talk about a lot of fun! The cooperative twist makes the game more challenging, funnier and kinder. It encourages ingenuity rather than ill will, teamwork rather than tantrums. The kids have fun without needing to dominate and decimate. They spend more time hugging than shoving. It's a great example of a simple change of focus bringing a huge shift in outcome.

It's interesting, isn't it, that from the earliest of ages we condition our children to understand that there have to be winners and losers, rather than showing them and championing cooperation. Kids love games, so it's just as easy to start playing cooperative ones as it is to play combative ones.

"After all, the initial impulse to play a game is social," says Jim. "That is, we bring out a game because we want to do something together. How ironic then that in most games, we spend all our efforts trying to bankrupt someone or destroy their armies—in other words, to get rid of one another! We soon learn how to pick on the other person's weaknesses in order to win the game."

So many people talk about why it's so important that kids play sport in order to develop 'character', but how many parents do you see on the sidelines who are peaceful, joyful and willing everyone to do well?

If kids think they're only playing the game to win, they miss out on all the fun in between the start and the final whistle. If kids think they have to claw their way to the top, they don't get to relax and enjoy the view along the way. I'm not talking about raising a bunch of softies; I'm talking about raising decent, caring, fulfilled people.

"Competition makes it difficult to share our skills, experiences and resources because each person is separately involved in his or her exclusive goal," says Jim. "In our schools and work places, students and employees are often taught to regard each other not as potential collaborators, but rather as opponents, rivals and obstacles to their own success. In cooperative settings, every person's role is important and valued. Individuality is respected, and concern for the needs of others fostered. The challenge shifts from 'striving to be number one' to working toward a mutual goal."

This doesn't mean you shouldn't encourage your children to aim high. They need to be able to be proud of their efforts. They need to achieve regularly. They need to reach for the stars. But it doesn't mean that achievement only comes from being the victor, from creating a loser.

Jim Deacove believes that 'cooperativeness' has been linked to greater learning and emotional maturity and strong personal identity. People who cooperate become more flexible in their thinking and are more willing to invent creative solutions. "The result is enjoyment, personal confidence and a feeling of self-worth. As your personal power grows, you get that 'I can make a difference' feeling."

Being a member of a sports team, debating team or dance group has lots of benefits, but membership also comes with responsibilities that you'll need to help your children deal with. Most competitive situations are full-on and stressful. Children can become agitated, anxious, and perhaps even aggressive. They're frightened of failure and when they're losing or not achieving their goal, they can feel tension, embarrassment and hostility.

Alternatively, cooperative activities such as building, gardening, repairing, cooking and helping are non-threatening and mostly non-judgemental (unless, of course, the food tastes terrible! ☺). "As a result, this creates an atmosphere for relaxation and wellbeing—the foundation for more genuine, healthy and playful fun," says Jim.

If your child goes to a regular school, the fact is that they're faced with competition each and every day—in a big way. As adults, we 'compete' for study opportunities, jobs and the opposite sex! Our efforts therefore need to be directed toward helping our children see that they only need to compete against their own best, their own goals. It shouldn't be about comparison with others, but about comparison with their own previous efforts. We also need to be opening their eyes to the benefits of cooperation, teamwork and sharing, for it's those attributes that will stand them in good stead as grown-ups. It's about getting on with people, not getting one up on them.

All children need to know that they're good at something in order to be able to build positive self-esteem, but they don't need to be good at something at the expense of others.

Daily within our own family we see competition, cooperation, selflessness and selfishness on a monumental scale. Psychologist and author Martin Seligman believes that it's whether couples can celebrate each other's successes, rather than how much they fight, that predicts the likelihood of divorce. So if we apply the same idea to siblings, there are many things we can do to help our children connect rather than compete as we guide them to a long-lasting, loving, lively relationship with each other.

We do this by letting our children know that just because we're making a fuss of one child, it doesn't mean we think any less of the others. We encourage them to take joy in their sibling's success, to celebrate the good stuff while reminding them of their own successes and encouraging them towards more. We try to demonstrate fairness by treating each child according to their unique personality, yet within the boundaries of family rules and expectations. That age-old child lament that "You love the others more than me" was quickly nipped in the bud in our house with the simple response "Well, you've all said that now, so it can't be true."

We'd be dreaming if we think kids can cooperate 24 hours a day though! Which is why we need to use our homes as a place where children can learn safely that life is all about conflicting needs and wants, and that compromise and communication are an everyday part of it.

It's hilarious really because our kids go through those torrid times when they're getting on each other's nerves...but do you think they'll walk away and get some peace alone somewhere? Nope! You can't even lever them apart. They need and want to be together, just as honey bees will cluster close in a hive for warmth, communication and just because it's what they do.

In the world of the future, these types of cooperative family ties will increase in importance once again, as circumstances mean we are forced to, or choose to, live closer to family members of different generations. Like honey bees, it will become crucial for family members to truly support each other in all endeavours, working and playing as a cooperative unit.

People will probably steer back to more connected families willingly, as we discover through tough times that big houses, high-profile careers, sporty cars, fair-weather friends and fabulous clothes are not always forever, and they definitely don't love you back. The knowledge that family members can be relied upon and 'have your back' gives peace of mind and a deep sense of contentment.

Not everyone has strong family ties with their own parents and siblings, but I think we all wish for this with our own children. Connection, not competition, is the way to go.

THOUGHT LAUNCHERS & CONVERSATION STARTERS

- Opt yourself and your kids out of a 'dog-eat-dog world' by exploring some **cooperative game** concepts.
- **Encourage your kids to join** some groups that don't have winning and beating others as the ultimate goal, perhaps a choir that visits retirement homes, Scouts or Girl Guides, environmental or volunteer groups.
- Cut out the competition; **don't compare** children's report cards, sporting prowess, abilities or physical traits.
- Deliberately provide your children with access to cooperative ideas, relationships and **role models**.
- If you are playing a competitive game, **model the difference** between gloating after a win and being humble.
- Teach your kids about **fair play**. When they play sport, encourage them to care about the other team. Simple things like helping the opposition up if they fall will make your children feel better about themselves than if they'd simply ignored that suffering!
- Try some sporting activities that involve a mix of **cooperation and caring**, like horse riding and rock climbing.
- If you and your partner have different opinions on a decision that has to be made, for example a major purchase, or going to an event, invite your children to a discussion where you and your partner both **state your case and resolve** your differences in a respectful rather than competitive manner. Let the children see how negotiations can take place without getting out of control. Show them the difference between competition and cooperation.
- Developing and maintaining **family traditions** is a great way to form ties that bind. Little sayings, secret gestures,

home movie nights and special Saturday-night suppers are all special connecting cells in the honeycomb of life.

- On a day when you've witnessed some great sibling interactions, **leave a note** in each child's room reinforcing how cool you thought their actions were.
- When your children are fighting, ask them to come up with a **peaceful resolution** to the conflict. It might be as simple as an apology, or five minutes in different areas of the house, or they may do a good deed for each other.
- Ask a child to help **surprise a sibling** once a week with a special treat.
- Increase the feeling of connection by planning some **fun family activities** where the focus is on everyone having a good time.
- **Compete TOGETHER** to achieve something, rather than competing against each other, for example: can we make a delicious dinner in less than 20 minutes? Can we surprise Dad by taking out the garbage without him seeing us doing it? Can we spring-clean the house in a morning and find 60 items to donate to charity?

Chapter 5

FAIRNESS

The community which has neither poverty nor riches will always have the noblest principles.

PLATO

Imagine you are at a potluck buffet and see that you are the first in line. How do you know how much to take? Imagine that this potluck spread includes not just food and water, but also the materials needed for shelter, clothing, healthcare and education. It all looks and smells so good and you are hungry. What will you heap on your plate? How much is enough to leave for your neighbours behind you in the line?

JIM MERKEL—RADICAL SIMPLICITY

Finally, I got it. After years feeling a little bit guilty about all that I had and all that I wanted, Jim Merkel's analogy above is what really woke me up. It spoke so much to me, and helped me realise that it's not just about having the money, the connections, the ability and the opportunity to consume, it's about understanding that many of the things we're using now—and take for granted—are already unavailable to many in the world, and will be available to even fewer—if to anybody at all—in the future. Simply speaking, it's about fairness.

In his book, *Radical Simplicity*, Jim Merkel, from the Global Living Project, talks about "taming our appetite" so we can live more harmoniously and equitably within the means of nature. But as anyone who's gone on a diet will tell you, unless your head is in the right place when you start, you'll feel hungrier than ever before and start gorging!

So, how do we get our kids—and ourselves—in the right head-space when they are used to and surrounded by so much? We can start by questioning how happy we really are with all the stuff we own and consume. We can acknowledge the glaring inequality of distribution of the world's resources...and decide to take less. We can explain the reasons why we won't be shopping for packaged treats anymore, and why we won't be upgrading our mobile phone or computer just because a new one has hit the market. We can choose to take the train on holiday rather than a plane. We can show our children fairness by giving up some of our own buying habits and by minimising our ecological footprint. We can help our children understand that every drop of non-renewable fuel used on their behalf now is a drop of fuel that will be unavailable to their own descendants. This isn't to make them feel guilty; it's just so they come to know the world has limits.

When our kids are playing weekend soccer, softball or other sports, most of us tell them to 'play fair'. We expect the other team to play fair too, and are outraged when it doesn't happen. And yet, if the world is the playing field, can you really look your children in the eye and tell them that your family is playing fair?

Being fair to others, even those we don't know and who haven't even been born yet, enables us to make positive changes in our daily lives. It's these changes that free our families up to enjoy a life of creativity, unfettered by overconsumption, clutter and costs.

It's certainly not plain sailing living with one foot in an over-consuming society and one foot in the fairer society we hope to transition to. We're faced with so many uncomfortable and challenging dilemmas. Do any of these sound familiar?

- Your family loves chocolate, but the Fair Trade blocks seem to be so much more expensive. And should you buy it anyway, given the environmental cost of shipping it such a distance? Or is it ethical to buy chocolate because it provides income to the poor people of the producer nation?
- You want your children to see, smell and touch an environmental wonder in the hope that by experiencing it, they will want to help protect it and will understand why you make 'sacrifices' in other areas of your life, but it requires polluting travel to get there. You feel torn between making family memories and making a donation directly to the cause.
- You want your child to be fit and active, so you say yes to organised sports that require lots of petrol-fuelled car trips and sport-filled weekends that don't leave much time for other hobbies, volunteering and down time.
- It's your child's birthday, and you want to go all-out and spend up on entertainment, decorations, party bags and gifts, and yet you wonder how much is enough. You want to make your child feel special, but you want to strike a decent balance.

What's fair? How fair do we have to be? Who do we have to be fair to? Can we still have fun? Well, of course we can still have fun—and probably loads more of it—but in relation to the other questions, you'll only be able to answer them over time, and through personal experience and effort. Everyone's answers will be different, and they will change over the years as you begin to live and breathe fairness.

It's okay to get it wrong too, especially if you learn from those mistakes. I've made huge whoppers in my quest to live a more sustainable life...and continue to! Just one was the time when, over a course of a few months, we had a surplus of milk from our goats. Unfortunately the government has draconian laws against home dairies sharing and selling raw goat's milk, so we drank lots, made cheeses, made soap, and even gave our daughter regular goat's milk baths to help with her eczema. The chickens were getting some excess, we were freezing it and more...and then I went and bought an ice-cream machine! What was I thinking?! At the time, I was thinking it would be so much better to make our own ice-cream with goat's milk than buy cartons from the store...I hadn't even questioned if we really needed ice-cream on demand!

Living fairly means that rather than living on autopilot, we consciously choose to take less and live on less. It's about treating the planet and its resources as though we are just borrowing them for a while and need to hand them back in better condition for others who come after us. With resource depletion, climate change and social and economic unrest though, one day soon it might not even be a matter of choice...our children will just **have to** make do with less.

Some people's reaction to the threat of a reduction in the quality of their lifestyle is to try and grow even wealthier so they can outbid others for needed supplies and luxuries, but if your aim is to treat others as you would like to be treated, you're more likely to be sharing than stockpiling.

'Abundance' is such a warm, hopeful, generous word, and when you share abundance, it's not only a fantastic feeling, but it can also set off a cascade of sharing and generosity with far-reaching, positive consequences. By sharing abundance, whether it's extra vegetables, some time, your craft, your humour, or your car, it encourages others to share their abundance as well...now if we can only get the government to change the laws about sharing abundant goat's milk!

I've found that children are especially open to sharing, volunteering, helping and championing needs, causes and individuals. It isn't second nature to everyone, but it takes just one young leader to open their peers' eyes to the fun and fulfilling nature of fairness and helping others, and boom—rather than youth inaction, you've got youth in action!

It's interesting and sad to see how this sense of charity and fairness can also be manipulated. Have you noticed the way some charities are becoming more and more corporation-like in the way they target children?

Our kids regularly come home from school saying if they raise a certain amount of money for a charity—by reading books or jumping a rope or selling chocolates—they'll receive all manner of rewards from wristbands to soccer balls to electronic games. Having worked for charities, I fully understand the difficulty of raising funds (especially as less and less support for the disadvantaged and sick comes from our governments), but this method is not about encouraging free giving and compassion in our children, it's about bribery.

Perhaps take the time to share with your kids the idea that if they really want to support a charity, they can raise the money but not ask for any type of reward for doing so. That way, even more money goes to the charity, and one less 'junk toy' needs to be produced at the expense of the planet and humanity. Ask them to consider that if once the rewards are taken out of the equation, they don't feel that strongly about a charity, maybe they should find a different one to support. There are so many wonderful charities out there working to bring fairnesss to the world and its different species, there will definitely be one your family can champion.

Encourage your children to think about fairness in their daily lives, their fairness to siblings, friends, animals, the environment and the billions of people they don't know. Show your own belief in fairness through your actions, too; that's the best example you can set!

Another way to think about fairness is to encourage your children from an early age to put themselves in different shoes. 'Treat others how you'd like to be treated' is a saying that seems to have been forgotten in the rush for the last toy on the shelf!

In beekeeping terms, if a beekeeper takes more than his fair share of honey from a hive, it puts undue stress on the bees and can cause the death of the entire colony. In human terms, it's vital we reassess our notion of fairness before the environmental, social and economic challenges of our time become too overwhelming to moderate. By encouraging fairness at home, in the community and when we're choosing what to spend our money on, global fairness can become a reality.

THOUGHT LAUNCHERS & CONVERSATION STARTERS

- Ask your children what they see around them in their day-to-day lives that **doesn't seem fair**. Ask if there's anything they think they can do about it.
- Contact a **charity** you like and ask them to add an option to their fundraising whereby a child can choose not to receive a reward for their efforts. Maybe the charity could send a photo of the person/animal/environmental area that they've helped instead of a plastic toy.
- Try to be fair at all times in your own family. If you've reacted badly on occasion, **apologise** to the kids so they can see another type of fairness in action.
- **Donate blood** regularly so your children can see that if you are able to give, the circle of life means that one day you may be able to receive also.
- Think about **things you do every day** and ask how fair it is to continue, e.g. how much oil is it fair to use in your life, knowing that once it's gone, no one else will ever have access to it.
- If your child is a **leader**, help direct him or her to doing community good, rather than just leading the gang from shop to shop, from hang-out to hang-out.

- Consider whether your choices are based on **mutual benefit** or exploitation.
- Think about whether it's fair to take good organs with you when you die, or whether they might be put to good use by donating them to someone who needs them. Discuss **organ donation** with your children, and see what they think about it.
- Have the kids come up with some 'Fair Rules to Live By' whereby they decide what is and isn't acceptable in their relationship, e.g. name-calling, taking toys without asking, etc. Then hold them to it; after all, they made and agreed to the rules in the first place! Update the rules every six months.
- Your children can begin contributing to a fairer world by starting **their own project** or joining with other children on established ones. Here are some sites you might like to check out with them:
- **Taking it Global:** www.takingitglobal.org, an online community of young people interested in global issues and creating positive change.
  - **Global Youth Action Networking:** www.youthlink.org. GYAN is a youth-led, not-for-profit organisation that unites the efforts of young people working to improve our world.
  - **I Buy Different:** www.ibuydifferent.org, a site that helps educate kids about how they can make a difference through their purchasing power.
- **UNICEF Voices of Youth:** www.unicef.org/voy/, provides information on what youth can do right now to help.
- **The Red Cross/The Red Crescent:** www.icrc.org. The International Committee of the Red Cross (ICRC) is an impartial, neutral and independent organization whose exclusively humanitarian mission is to protect the lives and dignity of victims of war and internal violence and to provide them with assistance. It directs and coordinates the

international relief activities conducted by the Movement in situations of conflict. It also endeavours to prevent suffering by promoting and strengthening humanitarian law and universal humanitarian principles.

- **Oxfam International:** www.oxfam.org. Oxfam is an NGO (non-government organisation) confederation of 13 like-minded groups working to improve the lives and livelihoods of poor people around the world.

Chapter 6
....
HEALTHY LIFE CHOICES

Time and health are two precious assets that we don't
recognize and appreciate until they have been depleted.

DENIS WAITLEY

It's bizarre that the produce manager is more important
to my children's health than the pediatrician.

MERYL STREEP

Health and quality of life are so intertwined that we're lucky that good health comes naturally to many of us. What's not so natural though are all the things we're eating, inhaling and absorbing that are leading many of us to suffer from preventable chronic diseases.

In the last few years we've seen a startling decline in the health of bees around the world. Investigations point the finger at potent mixes of pesticides and herbicides in use on the world's agricultural crops. Others believe genetically modified foods are part of a cocktail of woes that, alongside varroa mites, have led to an outbreak of an

AIDS-like syndrome in the honey bee. What's not in dispute is that Colony Collapse Disorder (CCD) has widespread implications for not only bees, but humans as well. I can't help but think that bees are the modern canary in the coalmine.

Health matters, not just as a personal issue, but on an immense social scale as well. When people are chronically ill, are diagnosed with a fatal disease, or just drop dead, the impact on society and nations as a whole is huge. There's not only a financial cost, but a huge emotional toll as well.

For the ill, there's the excruciating loss of their vitality, a loss that impacts their immediate family, and restricts their ability to positively impact on their community, environment, state and nation. Though some terminally ill patients are truly amazing and help rally community resolve and fund-raising, illness as a whole definitely diminishes rather than enhances lives.

There is financial loss to the family, whether that be due to loss of income, the cost of medication, or the rippling needs that illness causes. This financial loss spreads out through the community, borne by regular taxpayers who must maintain the system (and I say 'regular' tax payers because many corporations, multinationals and the wealthy have managed to minimise their tax bills so effectively that there's hardly any left to go back into the community health pot).

Then there is the loss we feel so deeply when friends and family leave us too soon, and in too much pain, the loss of community members who don't reach their full potential, the loss of the wisdom the long-lived accrue, or the premature loss of our young people's vitality.

However, all is not lost! We can aim for vitality for our children by choosing healthy food, actively avoiding carcinogens and toxins, by exercising and by doing good. It should be pretty simple really, but depending on our location, our socioeconomic group and our peers, it can feel like an insurmountable challenge.

Look, we've all got to die, but it's a tragedy to die of something that's totally preventable. That's why we have to be honest with our kids, and ourselves, about preventative health. We need to take responsibility for educating and taking care of ourselves to the best of our ability.

Do you know what scares me? It's the knowledge that some big businesses and government departments and even schools don't always seem to have our best interests at heart; that the juggernaut of product development and food additives just keeps rolling on, with no thought of the impact on human health or the environment, from processed foods to synthetically derived hair conditioners, air freshener sprays to insect repellents.

Take bottled water for example. At first we lapped up the marketing messages; healthy, fresh, better for you than tap water, easy and convenient. Yet look behind the liquid and we find immense landfill problems, pollution caused by the manufacture and distribution of the bottles, and scientists raising concerns about the hormone disruption tendencies of BPA (bishpenol phosphate), the material used to make the bottles. Luckily, there's a simple solution—have a nice long drink before you go out, or switch to reusable stainless steel bottles.

As parents, we need to look closely and do our research whenever we buy something. Read the packaging, and then read it again. If there's an ingredient you're not familiar with, do your own research, although sometimes not all the ingredients are even listed, as proven by a Friends of the Earth research report into cosmetics in 2009. The tests carried out by the Australian Microscopy & Microanalysis Research Facility found that seven out of 10 of the cosmetics they tested had 'penetration enhancers', ensuring that the nanoparticles used in the cosmetics could enter the bloodstream and be absorbed by organs and tissues. Friends of the Earth called these nanoparticles "the 21st century equivalent of lead and arsenic."

Now, take a look around you. What is there in the room that is natural, and what is artificial? Perhaps there are toxic halogenated fire-retardants in your cheap imported couch from China, or in your children's pyjamas. Maybe the paint on your walls is offgassing chemicals into the room, while you inhale VOCs (volatile organic compounds) from the lacquer on your bookcase. The carcinogen formaldehyde rises invisibly from the upholstered chair you're sitting on, while your children's airways and lives are being damaged by the textile dyes in their bedspreads. Erk. Don't cringe too much, though. Buy a book about healthy homes, get online, and read up so you're in a position to make decisions for the health of your family. While you're at it, get some more indoor plants to help filter the air!

We and our children are being bombarded by synthetic chemicals, but we can make some easy changes. Whenever possible, go natural! Choose simple over sophisticated. Choose basic over bling. Read up on chemicals and natural alternatives. Buy organic rather than processed. Make it yourself, or buy it from someone who can explain what natural products they work with. Choose a flyswat over flyspray. Own less, but own quality, pure items. There'll be less clutter in your house and more health, thanks to your nous!

When I started beekeeping, I'd collect the beeswax, filter it and melt it in a solar oven, and then store it. After a couple of years, I was ready to start using it, and the first thing I made was lip balm. Why lip balm? I researched the ingredients contained in famous brand lip balms and couldn't believe they were allowed to sell that stuff to us to put on our lips.

While most of the health threats to our children are actually legal, we also have to deal with the illegal ones. The topic of drugs is one that many parents avoid, because they're never quite sure when it's a good time to have the conversation. We want our children to be innocent, and yet we also need them to be informed.

In our family, we feel that childhood has become so compressed that drug-taking is affecting much younger kids now, so from a very early age, we've explained to our kids what illegal drugs are, the effect they have, what they might look like, and that the 'business' of drugs puts money in the hands of people you wouldn't want to shake hands with. We try to get them to think all the way back through the supply chain to see the pain and suffering drugs can cause, dispelling the notion that drug-taking is about being glamorous, independent and cool.

According to a report by Nick McKenzie and Dylan Welch published in the Sydney Morning Herald on 15 September 2010, one of the world's most powerful organised crime syndicates has infiltrated Australia. The cartel is based in Mexico, where more than 28,000 people have died since 2006 when the president ordered a 'drug war' against the cartel and its rivals in the drug trade. This shows that the human cost is not just in relation to the end user, but right back at the source, and up-and-comers in business suits in the high rises and trendy bars of Australian, British and North American cities have a direct hand in the violence being perpetrated on the other side of the world.

Sometimes when I hand out vitamin pills, I remind my children never to take pills from others, even if they're told that they're 'vitamins'. I tell them stories of people we know who have been affected by drugs, that marijuana isn't a safe drug and can have life-changing side effects for many, including inducing psychotic episodes and severe, permanent mental illness. My own brother died from a heroin overdose. Drugs kill. Drugs fund criminals. Drugs demean. Drugs divert. Drugs never solve anything. That's the message children need to hear, see and internalise. They'll also be able to avoid drugs if you let them know from early on that they can make their own fun and enjoy themselves without the use of chemicals. Just like a strong, healthy beehive is better able to fight off mites and disease, a strong and close relationship with parents is key to minimising the chances that your children will be side-tracked by drugs.

The best way not to be tempted by drugs is to avoid the people and places where they are prevalent. Easier said than done! You'll want your children to be able to say "no" without getting into an argument or losing face when they have peers or colleagues offering them a chance to get 'high', so practise showing them things they can say that will get them out of the situation without making them feel 'left out' or 'uncool'. Who knows what will work for them, but encourage them to think up ways of saying "no" that they'd be okay with, such as, "I can't, I've got to be up at six am tomorrow, I'm playing/going to/doing X," or "Thanks, but my uncle died of an overdose, so I'm pretty susceptible to that stuff," or "Thanks, but it's not my thing," or "Be my guest, but I'm playing sport tomorrow and I don't want to let my team down."

I know, some of these might sound a little lame, but unless you start offering some suggestions, your children might never think about how to say "no", which means they'll be more likely to say "yes" when they're put on the spot.

Health, vitality, longevity, happiness—our children won't experience these awesome states without a lot of work on our part and lots of self-respect on their part. As we head into uncertain times, with perhaps less safety nets, higher medical costs and more preventable illness than ever before, good health will be even more important to our children.

THOUGHT LAUNCHERS & CONVERSATION STARTERS

- Ask your children for their **ideas on how they can avoid** contracting diseases so they don't have to stay in bed sick when there's lots of fun stuff going on, e.g., healthy diet, hand-washing, avoiding toxins, etc.
- Encourage the kids take a look at the back of all the bottles in your house (shampoos, conditioners, liquid soap, washing powder, pest sprays) and ask them to identify the **natural ingredients** and the chemical ones. Give them some time on the Internet to research some of those long names so

they can try to work out whether they're safe or not. If they find that some are toxic, get them to agree to change to something safer.

- When the kids are haranguing you to buy them something from the junk-food aisle, have them read the **ingredients list** on the back of the object of their desire. Get them to read out the numbers, and then explain to them how each of those numbers is a chemical, and that you love them too much to let them put that stuff into their bodies. If you don't mind them having something every now and again so they don't think you really are a monster, have them find something similar but without all the numbers in the list of ingredients! Teach them what to look for so they can look out for their own health.

- Activity: next time you go to get groceries, show your children the list of ingredients on a packet of cake mix. Then shop for your own ingredients, and bake the cake. Have your children **compare the different number and type of ingredients**. Perhaps also discuss the packaging, energy and pollution involved with the manufacturing of the commercial cake mix.

- If your children are seven or older, they could be **cooking a meal each week** for the family. Let them choose what they'd like to cook, and give them the support they need, but let them take charge.

- **Speak honestly and openly** with your children about all the major issues they're facing, such as friendships, drugs or sex. If they learn early on that you can be trusted to tell them the facts, they'll keep coming back for more. Encourage their questions and be truthful.

Chapter 7

THE KITCHEN GARDEN

We abuse land because we regard it as a commodity belonging to us. When we see land as a community to which we belong, we may begin to use it with love and respect.

ALDO LEOPOLD

High-tech tomatoes. Mysterious milk. Supersquash. Are we supposed to eat this stuff? Or is it going to eat us?

ANNITA MANNING

Everything that slows us down and forces patience, everything that sets us back into the slow circles of nature, is a help. Gardening is an instrument of grace.

MAY SARTON

When the bees have filled the honeycomb and capped all the cells with beeswax, it's time to extract the honey. We scratch off the caps with a wire comb, using no heat so the honey stays perfectly raw like nature intended. Then we hand-spin three frames at a time in a stainless steel extractor. The honey flicks out onto the sides of the steel tank, running down the sides, passing through a filter and into the collection barrel. Our youngest daughter is always right on the spot to taste the first drop from the tap, and though we've been watching what trees and plants are in flower, we just never quite know what the honey is going to taste like. It might be light and taste like sunshine, or it might be thick and medicinal or mellow caramello! One thing's for certain; we know it's pure, we know it's healthy, we know it's good.

But what a minefield the whole area of food has become for our society: overweight toddlers, anorexic teenagers, yo-yoing yummy mummies, obese oldies, diabetic dads, not to mention polluting packaging, imported food with its own round-the-world air ticket, genetically modified meals, serious allergies, dwindling nutritional values, food shortages, starvation, preservative-laden, artificially coloured, certified organic...the whole thing sounds like a Mad Hatter's picnic.

In Greg Critser's book *Fat Land—How Americans Became the Fattest People in the World*, he writes about the US regulatory system for food, the USDA & the FDA, saying, "Then, as now, foods were lightly regulated; their long-term medical consequences were less important than their immediate safety, purity and usefulness."

This is a wake-up call for all of us who thought that, "If they're allowed to sell it, it must be okay." As our population struggles more and more with heart disease, cancer, serious allergies and diabetes, we need to concentrate much more on the types of food and the amount of food that we and our children consume.

The messages we give to our children about food last a lifetime, so let's give them clear, sound ones:
- Food is basically fuel for our bodies
- Healthy fuel means healthy bodies and happier people
- Healthy food needs to be grown in healthy soil
- The types of food you eat can help prevent disease

- You should be able to recognise and name all the ingredients in the food you eat (i.e. whatever was around in Grandma's day should be alright)
- Only eat when you're hungry (not when you're bored, sad, etc.)
- Stop eating when you're full
- Food that's grown, prepared and shared with love can be a wonderful thing.

My mother gave me another great message about food, and it's not what she said, it's what she didn't say. She never, ever, used the word 'diet' in our house. She never talked negatively about her body shape, even if she had her own problems with it. Therefore, I didn't even realise that you could have a problem with eating too little or too much or not being happy with your body type until I was well into my teens, and by then I'd missed the self-loathing boat.

She also preached a message of moderation, the words "everything in moderation" echoing (and echoing!) around our family dinner table. We were allowed fizzy drinks a couple of times a year on special occasions, and ice-cream or a lolly some nights, and we were never made to feel guilty when we enjoyed these pleasures, but we totally got the message that they were 'sometimes' foods, not 'all-the-time' foods. A doughnut at the shops was a once-a-year special, as was dinner out. For dinner, we ate recognisable food, close to its natural state.

Our children need to know that food that's closest to its natural state is the healthiest to eat and that means adding more raw, uncooked foods to mealtimes—cavemen didn't land on the earth with microwaves, that's for sure!

At the next level, you might take the example of a cake. A cake you make at home might use flour, eggs, sugar and butter, while a cake you buy might have all these ingredients as well as a huge amount of colourings, flavourings, fillers and preservatives. "Too many numbers," I often say to the kids after reading the list of ingredients on the back of product packaging in the supermarket. They know that means it's about to be put back on the shelf.

As any parent knows, mealtimes, no matter what the 'make mealtime fun' gurus say, can be battle zones. I don't know what happens in your family, but I constantly have to remind myself that I'm not doing the kids a favour if I put a biscuit in their lunch box instead of a banana.

It would be nice to think our kids always ate healthy and didn't crave and covet other kids' lollies, but that's never going to happen. They rock up to school, or parties, or visit their friends' houses and the choices put in front of them are supercharged with sugar, salt and fat and have more preservatives than an Egyptian mummy! You can't even recognise the ingredients because they've been so pulverised, blended, cooked, coloured, stripped, filled and manufactured that they could have started life as gravel. And yet this is what our kids seem to crave, covet and covertly consume.

I think many of us were happy to sign up for the job of 'parent' without realising that part of the job description was 'food warden'! Yes, being the chief health officer in the family can be hard work, but what we put into and onto our children's bodies really matters.

Stephanie Alexander of the Kitchen Garden Foundation believes that "by setting good examples and engaging children's innate curiosity, as well as their energy and their taste buds, we can provide positive and memorable food experiences that will form the basis of positive lifelong eating habits."

It can be hard to get kids to understand that we're fighting for them, not against them, especially if we let dinnertime arguments get heated, so for every food decision we make, we need to be able to explain in a loving way why our family has that rule. We also have to be prepared to be flexible. Sometimes, we may have a choice of five vegetables for dinner, and the kids only need to choose their favourite three to put on their plate. It's give and take, but it's a whole lot better than takeaway!

We try to teach the kids that what they put in their mouths is their best protection against disease; that it's like a suit of armour they wear on the inside; that yes, the packaged food may be tastier and trendier, but the closer to real food you can eat, the better it is, both for them and the environment.

When it comes to dessert though, no matter the pleading, no matter the drama, no matter the volume: they only get dessert if they've eaten the good stuff first.

We also need to be honest with ourselves that filling our cupboards with packaged 'treats' isn't doing our children any favours, nutritionally, financially or environmentally. Try replacing bought snacks with some wholesome homemade treats that the kids can make themselves!

One of the big questions these days though is even when we carefully select foods for our family, do we really know what we're eating?

Fran Murrell of MADGE (Mothers Are Demystifying Genetic Engineering) said in an interview with Necia Wilden of The Australian on April 30, 2011: "There's been a huge increase in food allergies in children since the introduction of GM foods here in the mid-'90s. The line we often get is, 'There is no evidence it's caused by GM.' But no one is investigating it. The fact is, there have been very few animal-feeding trials done on GM foods—those that do exist have often shown alarming results—and our own food safety regulator, FSANZ, relies on Monsanto (the US-based biotechnology company and leading producer of GM seed) to do its own safety testing. So of course we can't say for a fact that this spike in allergies is caused by GM, but we can say we're worried about it, and we have a right to be worried.

"And how can you trace illness to GM when the labelling is so inadequate? I think most people have no idea they're eating GM foods every day. They say they read the labels, but loopholes in our laws mean almost no GM ingredients require labelling."

There have been numerous studies done raising concerns about genetically modified foods. As parents, we should seek them out, read them, and share them with our friends and our elected representatives.

THOUGHT LAUNCHERS & CONVERSATION STARTERS

- Speak with your kids about making healthy choices. The approach that explains to children that foods can be divided between **'sometimes foods'**, 'all-the-time foods' and 'try-to-avoid foods' seems to be a simple way for kids to understand what's healthy for them to eat, and how often they should eat it.
- Next time you're at a restaurant, order the kids a bowl of **vegies for their starter** so they fill up on those before launching into their nuggets and chips!
- There's a role for **treats in moderation.** The real issue is that food should not be the only pleasure our kids experience. For example, make a list of non-food rewards like an hour with Mum doing craft, a hug, having a book read to them, having a friend over to play, going ice-skating, going to the park with Dad, etc., to show them all the other—often more natural and real—ways to get their happy vibes happening.
- Ask your children to come up with some phrases they can use to **turn down drugs** and alcohol and cigarettes.
- Ask your children to think about ways they could **convince a good friend** not to take drugs.
- Ask your children to decide if they think money is misspent or well spent on **elective procedures** like silicon implants, liposuction and other plastic surgeries. Ask them if they can think of a better use for the skills and time of doctors and medical facilities, such as discovering and disseminating

cures for as-yet untreatable diseases, or research that would help prevent asthma, etc.

- Young adults are more likely to die in a car accident than in a nuclear incident, so focus on the **day-to-day stuff** that will help them stay safe, like driving lessons!
- **Model the behaviour** you want to see in your children.
- How many **mirrors** are there in your house, and how large are they? If there are several, perhaps think about just keeping the one in the bathroom, as mirrors put so much focus on the individual, making us look inward rather than outward.
- **Enjoy a day building a cheap solar oven** with your children. There are plenty of plans online, and you'll have a cooker that has no ongoing fuel needs except sunshine.
- Look up some **raw food recipes** and go raw a couple of days a week.
- **Poor body image** is something that affects boys as well as girls, and men as well as women. It's easy to avoid some of the associated problems if you:

DON'T
- Allow your children to watch **music videos** that set up the body as the be-all and end-all.
- Buy **magazines** that focus on celebrity flab to fab crash diets, instant makeovers, gastric banding, botox and all those other quick-fix approaches to looking 'good'.
- Fill your cupboard with **junk** food.
- **Indulge** your children or try to make up for their disappointments through food.

and DO
- Feed your children healthy, **home-prepared**, nutritious food.
- Help them understand that they may as well get used to their base **body type,** because it's the only one they'll ever have.

- Discuss how much **energy** goes into creating food...from the sun to the soil to the farmer to the cook.
- Get your children **involved** in preparing meals...not just cookies!
- Visit www.madge.org.au and read some of the latest findings on **GM research** so you can better choose what to put in your shopping bag.

Chapter 8

GETTING DIRTY

*A garden is a grand teacher. It teaches patience
and careful watchfulness; it teaches industry and
thrift; above all it teaches entire trust.*

GERTRUDE JEKYLL

*A garden requires patient labor and attention. Plants do not
grow merely to satisfy ambitions or to fulfill good intentions.
They thrive because someone expended effort on them.*

LIBERTY HYDE BAILEY

*When gardeners garden, it is not just plants
that grow, but the gardeners themselves.*

KEN DRUSE

Whenever I take honey from the bees, I plant them more trees, herbs and flowers so they're surrounded by plentiful, year-round food sources. They love plants like basil, abelia bushes, sunflowers, lavender, cosmos, clover, borage and lots of native species. They like variety, and thrive when they're not forced to live off monocultures. It's a gardening loop, and just as gardening can enhance the lives of bees, it can enhance your children's lives too.

Gardening is a leisure activity that all the family can participate in. It builds a sense of community and contribution, encourages physical, healthy exercise outdoors in the sunshine that literally gives you fruit for your labour (and not chemically enhanced or GM fruit!), and is a life skill worth learning.

When Dr Maarten Stapper, a leading researcher and agricultural scientist, talks about the soil, he calls it "the skin of planet Earth." Right now, our Earth's skin is stretched so tight, is so cancerous in parts and so quickly flaking off in others, that it desperately needs you and your children to pay it significant attention.

It seems that we go through stages with our relationship with dirt. As kids, we love to play in it, and as adults we loathe it. We tend to scrub, launder and vacuum it, but we rarely think about or tend to it. That seems like a big error of judgement in relation to something so fundamental to life and growth and on which our health depends.

Good human health begins with the soil our food is grown in, but how many of us have ever expressed interest in the quality of the soil in which our broccoli, beef and beans have been grown? We're just not encouraged to make these connections. Sure, we're taught a little about food pyramids and food chains at school, but the soil sure doesn't feature at its base. It's as though our food grows magically in the thin, air conditioned air of a supermarket aisle.

Over the last century, our soils have been effectively mined of their goodness, stretched to their capacity by chemical fertilisers and depleted of healthy minerals and microbes. Our valuable topsoil—a resource for all humanity—has been exposed, concreted over, washed away during rainstorms and blown about by the wind during drought. Years of industrial farming with its lack of natural replenishment means plants, animals and humanity are no longer getting the best level of nutrition.

Do we have an obesity epidemic because our bodies are craving nutrients we're no longer getting, leading us to eat more and more to fill the gap? Are cancers striking more people, at younger ages, because our bodies have been filled with artificial and preserved foodstuffs and don't have the defences to fight back?

It's not okay for our children to be eating food that's been sprayed with chemicals that result in fish kills and the deaths of small species. It's not okay that our children's preferences are for foods with ingredients they can't recognise over those that they can, like breakfast cereal instead of pieces of apple, or snack bars instead of carrot sticks.

Fortunately, there *is* another way. And it's a fun one. It's called: teaching your children to garden.

If, like me, you've managed to kill pretty much every plant you've ever been given—even cactus—don't worry; there's hope!

Here's why knowledge of organic gardening is such a loving gift to share with your children:

- it provides healthy, nutritious, non-genetically modified or pesticide-laced, life-giving food
- it reduces your family's food miles and therefore pollution and carbon footprint
- it gets your children out in the fresh air and sunshine so they get their Vitamin D
- it gives you a healthy, physical, cooperative activity you can do together
- it saves your family money
- it teaches children the skill of growing their own food
- it puts you in touch with other like-minded people (perhaps you and your children can contribute to or start a community garden if you don't have space of your own)
- it helps develop children's observation skills
- it gives you a great way to compost your own kitchen waste

- it gives your children a connection to and a healthy relationship with the food they eat
- it makes them aware of nature and inspires an appreciation of the seasons
- it gives them an invaluable skill and affinity for plants for life
- it gives them an opportunity to earn pocket money if they sell some excess produce
- it gives them a sense of accomplishment knowing that they've helped put food on the table
- it teaches them the philosophy of seed-saving so they will always be able to select the best seeds for planting the next year. (This ability to save and grow a wide variety of heritage foods means they won't need to rely on the hybrid varieties owned and controlled by some of the world's largest companies.)
- it will give them food security in the increasingly insecure food chain.

Before you say you don't have a green thumb, that's okay—hardly anyone does. No one expects any new skill to be gained overnight, and yet some kind of mythical status abounds about green thumbs, which is a shame, because I think it discourages many people from giving gardening a real go. It gives them an excuse not to try.

Think about it: we don't expect people to become expert veterinarians, teachers or hairdressers overnight, yet we seem to think that if we kill a few pot plants, we'll never be able to grow a lettuce to save ourselves. Not true. To be able to grow some of your own food doesn't require a degree in botany; it just requires your commitment to experimentation and learning.

If you don't already have a vegie patch, here's a chance to be your children's best teacher as you learn together. Start by getting a good book on organic gardening—and I push organic here because now is not the time to be teaching your kids to garden with man-made chemicals that cost money and can affect their health.

If you're in a rental property, only have a small balcony, or aren't ready to rip up your lawn just yet, start small with container gardening. Cherry tomatoes, herbs, garlic and onions are a good place to start. A friend of ours who rents bought a second-hand trailer that he uses as the family's garden bed. That way, they can take it with them should they have to move.

You might also want to find out if there's a community garden in your neighbourhood where you can get a plot, and gain a lot of pals along the way as you work side by side. If there isn't one close by, pester your council until they set aside some land for you and start your own.

Now, kids being kids, they won't always want to work in the garden with you, so it's up to you to make it either fun, or just part of the weekly activities your family does together. We let our kids pick the seeds they want to plant based on the vegies they like to eat, so for the past few months there's been a blizzard of snow peas! They plant, tend, harvest, weigh, eat them and sell the leftovers to us.

Get together on a sunny day and discover the jobs they enjoy the most. It might be digging or watering or bug catching, and you can join in and do the stuff they don't like. Over time, they'll learn about gardening just by being with you. They'll learn to identify good and bad bugs, they'll learn what causes yellowing of leaves and they'll learn the perfect time to pick the produce. Above all, they'll learn that they can actually do it and produce a satisfying, tasty result, rather than spending another bland, unproductive 20 hours in front of the TV!

The garden is a great place to compost your kitchen waste. Your children will just naturally absorb the message that when you take something out of the soil, you need to put something back in. In this instance, recycling leads to healthier soil and means less waste on its way to landfill.

If you don't have room for a compost bay, or if you have a problem with vermin, a worm farm can also be a great source of fun and learning for your kids. It will markedly reduce the amount of 'waste' your family throws out: worms will take care of most scraps, paper and hair (but no animal by-products or citrus), and will provide you with wonderful fertiliser that can be diluted and used on your garden.

In our house, our eldest daughter owns the worm farm, as it was something she requested for her birthday. She also asked for a book of 1,000 baby names as she planned on naming each and every one of the little slitherers! She's even sold some of her special 'worm juice' to other local gardeners.

Organic gardening is a healthy activity. It provides physical exercise, it delivers a place uninterrupted by television or computers where you can hold a conversation, and it provides a huge amount of contentment in return for the effort you put in. Eating your own produce is definitely a feelgood moment, and sharing that produce with others is immensely fulfilling. Your children can be a part of that.

The vegetable garden is also an ideal place to teach your children about life. Old-time sayings like 'You reap what you sow', 'All things grow with love', 'From feast to famine' and 'Nip it in the bud' suddenly have meaning. Your children learn first-hand that they must put in effort in order to be rewarded, a wonderful lesson in a society where so many seem to think they're owed a living, lifestyle or solution.

I'd never had first-hand experience of that other old saying 'Putting one's roots down' until we moved to our current home at Honeycomb Valley Farm. For work and other reasons, we moved seven times in the first 10 years of marriage, so I'd never felt that we would be in one place long enough to make it worth planting a garden (and I didn't know then about dwarf fruit trees that you can grow in pots, portable garden beds and the like that you can take with you when you move), but finally, it all makes sense. We've planted trees, some of which will take up to 15 years or more to fruit. We've planted trees that will feed our grandchildren (here's hoping they like carob!), and in just three years we've already eaten our first apples, guavas, pecans and pomegranates. Now I know what it means to put roots down; it means to make the effort, to connect with the land and the place, to look toward a positive future for your family, and to settle in with your community.

And what about 'Making hay while the sun shines'? Your children will learn that putting things off isn't a wise decision. If they delay watering their watermelon vine, it will wither. If they put off plucking the caterpillars from the cabbage, there won't be any coleslaw. If they don't harvest the tomatoes, the birds will do it for them.

They'll also learn about the scarcity and abundance of the harvest, about good seasons and bad seasons, about giving and receiving. About having a backup and not relying on just one crop, and about the wisdom of 'not having all your eggs in the one basket'.

Sometimes, as families dash from the shops to sport, from work to dining out, it's easy to forget that sometimes we can be most content and productive in our own backyard.

THOUGHT LAUNCHERS & CONVERSATION STARTERS

- **Involve your children** in beginning or extending your production of fruit, vegetables or herbs. Work out where in your garden or on your balcony you'll get started, and what kind of containers or garden beds you'll use.
- Ask your children what vegies they would like to grow. Would they like to **start with herbs** they can put on pizza and garlic bread, or do they like fresh beans or cherry tomatoes as snacks? How about blueberries or oranges?
- Encourage your children to think about how they might **share, swap or sell excess produce**. A third, a third, a third

is a good way to divide it, as it teaches them about barter-ing, charity and commerce.

- Do some **research** about soil, organics, permaculture and biodynamics, and let that research guide you in your choice of fertilisers and pest control.
- Start meeting your **neighbours,** and set up a gardening co-op whereby each backyard is used to grow different foods to share, e.g., one family might grow carrots and onions, another family silverbeet and cabbages, etc. Then the next year you can rotate garden beds so the soil stays healthy and you gain experience growing different crops.
- Ask the kids to list 20 of their favourite names for **worms.**
- Discover some **farmers markets** nearby and pay them a visit, ask questions, and get to know your food growers.
- Suggest that you will purchase two-thirds of your **children's garden produce** for the family, but the other one-third they will need to gift in return for garden rent and being a part of the family.
- Spend an afternoon making a small **scarecrow** together, then have a family movie afternoon watching *The Wizard of Oz,* or act it and sing it yourselves.
- Take a holiday in an area that has **'pick-your-own' farms** so your kids can experience the fun of filling up a basket with fresh strawberries or other fruits and vegetables.
- When you're travelling, stop at roadside **farm-gate** stands and let the kids choose what to buy.
- Visit a library and borrow some books on **herbal medicine.**
- If you're looking for a charity to support, perhaps fund long-term solutions by assisting charities in developing countries that believe in teaching people about **sustainable agriculture.**

Chapter 9

MEANINGFUL WORK

By filling one's head instead of one's pocket, one cannot be robbed.

CHINESE PROVERB

Choose a job you love, and you will never have to work a day in your life.

CONFUCIUS

Jitters in the financial system have made many of us worry for our own jobs, but what are the prospects for our children? It's doubtful that being able to play a video game for four hours straight or apply make-up perfectly will be high on the list of skills your children will need in the future. And industries that are big employers today may well be employing far less people five, 10, or 20 years from now. Just look at what happened to the auto industry in 2009; massive layoffs occurred in an industry once seen as the 'driver' of the economy. That's why it's important to be open to the different types of jobs and skills that will be needed in the future, so you can help your children discover and prepare for them.

Many of us have preconceived notions of what a 'good' job is. We've gobbled up the garbage that a high-paying job automatically makes us happy. Family history and white-collar/blue-collar snobbery blinds us to career choices that may well suit our children more than the ones we desire for them. And we stubbornly (or ignorantly) act as though the world we live in today will be the same as the world of tomorrow.

I think kids are a great radar for the types of jobs that will still be promising in the future, because if a five-year-old can understand what you do for a job, then it's probably worth doing, e.g., "I grow food for people to eat", "I help fix broken bones", "I repair bikes." Alternatively, if it's too complicated to explain easily, maybe it won't be such a great career option, e.g., "I trade derivatives", "I invent chemicals to create a 'natural' flavour that's really synthetic", "I help people get money that their Aunty specifically asked them not to have when she died", etc.

Although in the past being a banker, property developer or lawyer might have been some people's way to financial riches, it doesn't necessarily mean that's still the case, or that it will always be so.

Thinking about the impacts of the scenarios discussed earlier, we might predict that there will be a decline in graphic design jobs, but more jobs dealing with graphic emergencies. We can see that opportunities in natural resources might be more promising than those in human resources, and there might be a growing need for generalists like general practitioners and bookkeepers over specialists like lap-band surgeons and futures traders.

Peak oil would mean that the most needed pilots might be those of rivers and harbours rather than those of the air. Sustaining the world's growing population will fall to real farmers, not data farmers. Marketers might wish they'd studied market gardening, not predictive analytics!

Bees are amazingly capable creatures. One of the reasons I'm so fascinated by them is that worker bees are able to fulfil so many roles in the hive during the course of their lives. From cleaning the honeycomb cells after the birth of a new bee, to navigating great distances, to guarding the entrance to the hive, to lifting more than their own bodyweight, they're remarkable all-rounders. And they're capable. They're not defined by being good at one thing, but by being good at many things. I can't help but think that when our children become adults the world will be easier for them if they can turn their hand to a variety of tasks.

At their most basic, the jobs we do are meant to fulfil key human needs, and yet during the last century it seems many have been created to satisfy indulgences, indulgences which most humans and the environment can no longer afford. Yes, we need food, but do we need over-packaged confectionery concoctions? Yes, we need water, but does it need to come in a plastic bottle from Fiji or France? Yes, we need shelter, but does it need to be in the form of a massive blockbuster with a three-car garage? As all these indulgences are wound back, be it voluntarily or involuntarily, many people will find previously booming industries heading into decline.

Water is a primary human need, so careers in the areas of finding, storing, moving, conserving, recycling and charging for it will increase in demand as more of the extreme scenarios come into play. Careers to benefit might be those of the hydrologist, plumber, dam-builder, bore-sinker, tank and pipe-maker, irrigation expert, weather forecaster and scientist. Conversely, careers in industries reliant on cheap water will be negatively affected.

Right now, small farmers are stretched to breaking point as they try to compete with imports, big business, increasing regulation and the rising cost of inputs like water, but food is definitely a crucial need. So when the consumerism bubble bursts, the long-term future of horticulturalists, farmers, cooks, botanists, homemakers, vets, farmhands, scientists and entomologists seems secure. People will always need to eat.

Shelter is our next need, so the skills of builders, woodsmen, labourers and carpenters will always be useful, but perhaps you shouldn't plan on much growth from industries focusing on fashion rather than functionality.

Our need for safety, security and health will see more opportunities for doctors, herbalists and proponents of natural medicine, emergency workers, security guards, nurses and carers. And if I put my gloomy glasses on, there'll always be the armed forces trying to snap up your child.

There will be exciting opportunities in alternative fuels and energy, and scavenging and recycling services as we try to reclaim all those precious minerals and metals we threw out with our electronics garbage. Cottage industries will spring up as families and groups work together to produce items on a smaller rather than a gigantic far-off factory scale. Functionality will take over from fashion!

A few years back, a strange thought (yes, one of many, as you've probably come to realise) popped into my head: what would happen if I were to be transported back to the Middle Ages? How useful would I be? The answer, of course, would be not at all. Zip. Zero. Nada. I would have been the 'less' in useless. How about you?

Sure, I could tell them about electricity, but could I generate any? No. Sure, I could tell them about what engines did, but could I explain how they worked or build one? No. And they would hardly have needed my extensive computing and driving skills!

I fall down in other key areas too. For example, I don't know how to start a fire without matches, even though I've seen them do it on *Survivor*. I don't have first-hand knowledge of how to collect or purify water, or preserve vegetables. I don't know how to help someone give birth (even though I've given birth!) and I don't know how to build a decent shelter from available materials. But I'm in the process of learning all these things, and I'm involving my kids in this learning too. A while ago I didn't even know how to properly care for wounds and ulcers, except to clean them and slap on a bandaid or antiseptic solution, but now I know that nectar the bees collect from the flowers of the tree *Leptospermum scoparium* (known as jellybush in Australia and manuka in New Zealand) turns into a honey that is fab for this. Being open to learning is the first step!

It's great to encourage our children to tinker physically with items, skills and crafts, as well as mentally with ideas and dreams and their own big picture. So many of us have lost the art of tinkering. Perhaps that's because its loss suits the 'modern' economy in so many ways. After all, businesses prefer us to buy new things rather than fix what's broken, they prefer us to buy in a box what we would otherwise create and construct ourselves, they prefer us to pay people to do things we could really do ourselves.

In the future, we might all be doing a whole lot more tinkering. It's possible that work might become more centred around providing for one's own family through direct action. That is, instead of our adult children going off to work in an office tower so they can afford to build a house, pay for nannies and buy food, they will actually partake more in the building of their own house, the care of their own children, and the growing of their own food. In addition, they'd be producing some excess produce, skills or services to trade with others in the local community. This vision would see more of us being generalists rather than specialists, and it would mean that we'd need to be much more adept at finding solutions with our hands and heads than finding a replacement online. It's strange, in today's culture, to think this might be so, but more and more people seem to be downshifting and doing just this, and if just some of the world's threatening scenarios come to pass, our children might have no option.

Our children will have more options though when it comes to separating their career from their personal identity. In today's culture, many of us evaluate and judge a person based on their career choice. The first question asked at parties is often "What do you do?", not "What are your interests?", or "What do you like to do?"

Start sharing with your kids now that what they want to 'be' when they grow up doesn't have to be answered with a career choice, but with the way they really want to be: fun-loving, caring, spontaneous, courageous, loved, useful, etc. What they want to 'do' as an adult explains their career choice, e.g., "I want to rescue people", or "I want to write stories", or "I want to be an entrepreneur" or "I want to work from home and be near my family."

How much do your children know about what you do for a living? I think it's hilarious and charming that although I hold down a couple of different jobs from beekeeping to balm-making to public speaking, because I work from home on the farm, my son tells everyone that "she's just my mum but she's very eco."

Do your children respect the work that you do? Do you? Is it a job within an industry that will benefit their generation, or is it one that will leave them with a mess to clean up? Is it a job that's good for their health, their body image, the air they breathe, the community they live in? If not, would you think about moving to a company that makes you proud, or to a role within your current company where you can champion fresh ethics, and influence environmental and product changes for the better? Do you have a job that you think matters? If not, maybe think about finding or creating a new one so you can devote your time, passion and smarts to it!

For years, I loved my city job, but one day, during a meeting in their funky boardroom on the twentieth floor, I reached a key turning point. There were 10 of us around the table, bright, passionate, focused...focused on marketing a multi-national's new chocolate bar to 8- to 12-year-olds. We were coming up with so many creative ideas the kudos was flying. Then my unborn second child kicked. And it all clicked.

The cold, hard truth about the fabulous career that I got a buzz from; that I spent two hours a day commuting for; that paid my mortgage, my toddler's day care bills and for holidays became startlingly clear in that moment. Like many people, I am passionate about fresh food, fresh air, fair play, family and furry things, and yet I was using my education, creative talents and days on earth to manipulate impressionable young humans to pester their parents to spend hard-earned money. And not on something vital or even useful, but on a food that resembled nothing found in nature and that was damaging to teeth and body—and the environment, thanks to its manufacture, plastic wrap and shipping around the globe.

Damn. Clearly an irreconcilable clash between my values and my vocation! So I quit, and after the initial fear and trepidation, began a journey of real discovery, which has led to this book.

If you don't feel you have the knowledge to embark on a new career—find a mentor! Or if you love what you do—be a mentor! Mentoring is a long-lost art that's ready for a comeback.

When I finished my first beekeeping course I didn't feel confident enough to care for a colony myself. I was worried that I'd have 50,000 bees on my hands and I'd kill each and every one of them through lack of skill, so I sought out a mentor, and Rod Blatch, aka the Bee Man, came to my rescue. Patiently, generously and in his own inimitable style, he passed on not only his deep love of and reverence for bees, but also insights only someone with decades of experience can develop. Imagine what a mentor could do in your life, or in your children's lives, and how it might impact your family's future.

Having worked for much of our own lives, we've probably come head to head with the fact that although some jobs provide a comfortable lifestyle, they might not provide for a worthwhile personal or family life. Hopefully we'll be able to support our children, through exploration, education and seeking out mentors so they can find an independent living that fits their calling.

THOUGHT LAUNCHERS & CONVERSATION STARTERS

- If your daughter loves ballet, **involve** her in making the costumes to teach her the skill of sewing. If your son loves football, help him improve his fitness by having him help with work in the yard. If your children like to fiddle, open up the hood of the car and let them fiddle with an engine. If you need a kid-sized table, get them to help you make it.

- Encourage **grandparents** to pass on skills to your children, skills such as quilting, baking, sewing, spinning, weaving and the use of hand tools.

- Work out ways to involve your children more in your work day so they can **witness first-hand** and learn from the commitments you make and keep each day, and learn from your struggles and achievements.

- Ask your children how they'd like to **earn a living** when they grow up. Get them to list 20 different things they might like to try.

- Come up with a list of ways your family could **earn money together** separate from your main work.

- Think about your current job and company. Is it where you want to be, or something you enjoy telling your children about? If not, can you make it so, or can you build a new career for yourself in a different company, or one of your own making, that you can be proud of, and **proud to share with your children**?

- Are there areas where you can **cut costs** in your daily lifestyle so you don't need to work so hard, or so that you can devote time to your own business and family?

- Is there someone you would enjoy **mentoring** or being mentored by?

Chapter 10

HOME IS WHERE THE HEART IS

Buy land, they're not making any more.

MARK TWAIN

Mark Twain said that more than a century ago. If only he knew how high the stakes were now, and how high mortgages are!

Land and housing; there's nothing quite like the feeling of having a place of your own...except perhaps the feeling many of us are yet to experience—that of actually paying it off! Unfortunately though, the paying-it-off part takes up much of our lives, causing great stress while draining our time and our relationships. So what messages should we be giving our children about housing? Will all houses in a certain price bracket be equal in the future?

Back in 1854, Henry David Thoreau wrote of the irony that people so willingly dedicated their lives to paying off a house only to find that their life was practically over by the time they'd finished. He pondered the necessity of a large house with its accompanying large debt, compared with the cost of a much more modest abode. If only he could see what we're faced with now! Unless you're prepared to join forces with others, build your own modest shelter and live in shared housing or an 'intentional community', home ownership costs continue on their northerly trajectory. But we have to live somewhere.

Many of us probably feel stuck where we are because we have the millstone of mortgage or rental payments around our neck, or because we want to live near family or work opportunities. Perhaps your home's value has fallen or you're struggling to pay it off on reduced incomes. Perhaps you actually love where you live, and would never want to move.

This chapter is not so much about where you are now, but about identifying the types of housing that might offer additional opportunities and peace of mind for your children in the world of the future.

Jim Merkel, in his book *Radical Simplicity,* writes, "Global living doesn't attempt to impose limits on others. It doesn't necessarily advise one to escape to the country or move into compact urban cubicles. It seeks to inspire our creativity, our ability to see that there are infinitely satisfying lifestyle packages compatible with living on a finite, equitable share of nature. Global living seeks to give you the tools to be the architect."

He's right, there are so many different options out there, but if all you've ever known is conventional living, you might not even have started thinking about alternatives.

Take your $500,000 suburban house in an outlying development. Typically, it's a big house on a small block, with plenty of room for a big-screen TV, but not so much for a vegie patch. The only way out is with a car, as public transport is pretty much nonexistent, or too crowded to contemplate.

Or the $500,000 designer apartment reached only by elevator, and with windows sealed shut to ensure that the building's air conditioning works well.

Or the $500,000 ground-level apartment right near the centre of town and within walking distance of a community garden.

Or the $500,000 farm, regularly suffocated by dust storms after years of over-farming, the riverbed long dry thanks to upstream irrigators.

Or the $500,000 hundred-acre forested plot with a natural spring and room to grow your own building materials like clumping bamboo and reeds for thatch, not to mention the great clay soil for shaping into bricks.

Or the $500,000 small acreage, with enough space for a wood-lot and to run some animals, plant an orchard and grow vegies.

Or the $500,000 well-insulated suburban house with the lawn given over to vegetable planting with integrated chicken runs, tank-fed irrigation systems and lots of potted fruit trees that can be moved indoors in winter. Cycleways outside link you to neighbouring suburbs.

Or the $500,000 intentional community title land where twenty families are able to share the purchase price and build their own abodes, sharing communal facilities like meeting areas, laundry, guest rooms and orchard.

Each costs the same to begin with, and yet clearly some may offer a better long-term option than others for your children in this changing world.

In the bee world, you're probably familiar with the standard-shaped hive. It's a rectangular box, normally painted white, and they can be stacked atop each other. This style is called a Langstroth Hive, and it's the type used by most beekeepers. Beekeepers use this style of hive because they're transportable, offer a commercial quantity of honey and, well, it's what everyone else is using! But there's also a modern-day move to a more natural type of beehive called a "Top Bar" hive, which allows the bees to draw out the honeycomb in the same shape as they would in the wild. So rather than the human-designated rectangular shape, as in the Langstroth Hive, the bees are able to build a long, drooping honeycomb that suits them better. This type of beehive also allows the bees to make honeycomb cells of different sizes as they see fit, which can help them manage the health, wealth and progeny of the hive better. Different housing options, different outcomes.

But it's not just the type of property that matters; it's where it's located. Bees like a nice sun-facing spot, near a water supply and with a little shade for the heat of summer. If their house burns down or is invaded by vermin, they move on. As for humans, well, we're harder to please!

It seems like the news is regularly overflowing with stories of people like you and me being affected by fires and floods, fearsome storms and torrid droughts, heatwaves and tsunamis. But how many of us are learning from the increasing frequency and ferocity of these events?

If part of your town has been razed in a forest fire, it might seem that staying and rebuilding shows resilience, but does it? If a fire can kill hundreds in the space of a few hours, what might an even fiercer fire do in that same area 15 years from now when the undergrowth has regrown and stretched governments are unable to throw the resources at the fire or pay for the community to be rebuilt? Lightning does strike twice. So is it resilience, or just a reluctance to face the truth? Is it easier for people to stay with 'the devil you know' rather than go through all the effort and emotional upheaval of relocating? I suppose the real question is, does it make sense? Can the dwelling be made safe? Are the people prepared to lose everything, perhaps even the lives of loved ones, again? It's easy to become attached to a building, a particular area, and special memories, but if that area can kill you—is the image romantic enough for you to want to stay?

There was a story on CNN about a town that had cancelled school so its residents could band together to build a sandbag blockade for miles and miles to keep out rising floodwaters; all very admirable, a fine show of human spirit and cooperation. Huge numbers of trucks and earthmoving vehicles danced in the distance, scooping, ferrying and building. They looked like mechanical ants preparing for a storm. I felt terrible for the people, their fear, and the potential for them to lose everything. Then the reporter announced that less than a decade ago, the town had been totally flooded, and though that one had been devastating, this one would be even worse. What a waste of non-renewable building material, fossil fuel, time, emotion and energy.

Ask your children if they think it makes sense to spend all their life savings and hefty annual insurance premiums on a property that has the potential to be wiped off the map every couple of years? Think about the increasing severity and frequency of such events with climate change, think about what rising oil prices will mean to the cost of such disaster-prevention measures. Will they still be feasible, or will whole towns simply be abandoned to their fate? Will the saying 'safe as houses' remain true? Or will we learn from the past and either avoid certain areas or construct cheaper, smaller, portable eco-housing so losses are minimised?

The weather forecasters talk about 'one-in-100-year' events, peak flood levels and record temperatures. Well, find out what these were in your area, because you can reliably expect them to happen again someday, possibly sooner rather than later!

I'm writing today as the rain comes down. A town three hours north of us has just experienced 700 mm of rain in 24 hours! The previous record was 270 mm. Cars are floating past shops, animals have been washed away, and people are being rescued from trees.

Ask your children to think about the type of weather that they enjoy the most and that is the most liveable. Sure, they might like skiing, but discuss with them the resources it takes to keep warm, grow food and survive in that type of environment. Have them think about their habitat.

Do you want to be living in a tropical paradise? Do you want to be living only a few feet above sea level? Do you want to be living on the edge of a massive forest? Of course you do, now. After all, the most expensive houses have views of the water, the thought of fresh air and peace draws us to the forests, and the balmy climates of the tropics seem to keep us in holiday mode all year round.

Trouble is, climate change wisdom is telling us there's going to be an increasing likelihood of serious weather events. Those languid tropics are prime storm zones, rising sea levels will potentially give you water views beyond your wildest dreams, and as for living on the edge of a tinder-dry forest...you get the picture. Rivers are great, but make sure you're well above the 100-year flood level... *well* above.

But how do you want to help your children prepare for the future? It may be time to pull out some maps of your local area, and areas further afield, and ask your children questions about what makes a place the best one to call home.

Of course, if you ask a four-year-old, they'll tell you they want a gingerbread house with lots of fairies in it. If you ask a teenager, they'll tell you they want an MTV Crib. Well, that's okay! At least you've got them thinking.

Given the realities of the world in which we're likely to be living, my husband and I have made huge steps toward creating the place we call home, yet if we were able to start from scratch, here are the attributes that we would investigate more:

- simple, durable construction and materials so it doesn't cost the earth—literally—and so it lasts a number of lifetimes
- easy to repair with materials close at hand
- designed to sit at the correct angle on the land, making it cooler in summer and warmer in winter, and with excellent natural light and breezes
- made of eco-friendly building materials with no use of toxic paints or carpets or other off gassing materials
- smaller rather than larger to allow for efficiency of heating and cooling, and to keep it small on floor space so as to allow for more productive gardens...but also a flexible floor plan so rooms can be added as needed for different generations to share
- a cellar built just off from the house for food storage and shelter in the event of fire

- water tanks to collect roof run-off, with a simple pump on a well or cistern
- non-toxic vermin- and pest-proofing to ensure the health of our family and security of our food stores
- a good wood stove with cooking facilities and a solar oven for outside
- as many built-in storage spaces and as much built-in furniture (such as seats along the walls) as possible so there is no need to buy extra furniture
- a waterless, composting toilet to ensure water conservation and ensure that fertility removed from the soil by food consumption is replaced.

And if I could choose the perfect piece of land on which that dwelling would be built, it would either be in a small city with great public transport, cycleways, open spaces, community gardens and waterways, or it would be on the outskirts of a country town and have the following attributes:

- enough space to grow fruit trees (even if only dwarf or in pots) and vegetables, with chickens integrated in garden bed rotation (i.e., move the chickens on to spent garden beds so they can eat weeds and bugs, while fertilising the plot getting it ready for the next planting). Even better if it had the space for a goat or two, not only for milk and cheese and to keep the weeds down, but also because they're delightful companion animals!
- positioned at least 30 metres above sea-level to avoid sea level rises: n.b., if you're paranoid, 90 metres might give you even more peace of mind, given that's the level that is quoted in the absolute disaster-case scenario should all the world's land ice sheets melt at once...but then there'd be plenty of other problems to worry about!
- positioned in an area with a moderate climate and good rainfall

- near a fresh water source like a spring or a creek, but not right on the banks of a major river or floodplain
- relatively close to a transport system that could run without conventional fuel, such as on a harbour or river, or perhaps an old train line would be in service nearby
- close to a community with services such as schools, doctors, dentists and the arts
- within financial reach so it doesn't take a lifetime to pay off
- with room for a woodlot, orchard and gardens.

Obviously, not everyone has the desire to leave the area of their birth or move to a rural location, so if that's you, there are still properties in your area that will be of more benefit to you and your family in the future than what presently might be the hot real estate in town. Beach and riverside apartments that still command big bucks will likely not be a suitable habitat to pass on to your children, but perhaps a large block with a small house will be.

For people for whom a mortgage is not within reach, rather than renting a place on your own, perhaps find the area in which you'd eventually like to put down roots. You may even connect with an elderly resident whose house is large and who may appreciate a renter to help with care and security in return for cheap rent. That way, you can start getting to know your intended community. One day, you'll be able to afford a place of your own, even if you do it by pooling funds with a sibling, a cousin or other family members, or by taking a long-term lease on an old cottage down the back of someone else's property.

And don't forget cooperative housing and intentional communities, where a set number of people purchase land and build dwellings on it, with shared features and benefits such as a dam, an orchard and gardens. As you're a part-owner, you could get started this way well before you'd be able to finance your own property independently, and you get an instant community to boot.

Thanks to cheap oil, we've been able to explore far and wide, and distance ourselves from our roots. The price to return to visit relatives has been a negligible few hours in a car or on a plane. As that changes, we'll need to think much more about where we want to base our families—and stay there. This will have an enormously healthy effect on the community in which we live, as we'll be more likely to take an interest and a role in the local social, political and environmental landscape.

In the West, different generations living together has previously been frowned upon in favour of privacy, independence and individuality. Our ability to live away from our parents, siblings and extended family was really only enabled by the mobility provided by cheap and abundant fossil fuels, cheap food and cheap furnishings.

Was the distancing of family perhaps even encouraged by business and government as a way of achieving economic growth? After all, it's much more profitable to sell three fridges to three small separate households. Ditto house and land packages, cars, telephones, beds, televisions…the shopping list goes on.

If you think about it, where are all the government and social policies aimed at helping even married couples stick together, let alone families? Has divorce been enabled by economics? Has separation flourished alongside the Super Centres? Who has benefited, and who has picked up the bill from wrecked relationships, tumultuous childhoods and gated-community grandparents?

It will be interesting to see, as mortgages skyrocket and the ability to pay them off plummets, if there's a small return in the West to married couples really working at marriage, generations bunking in together to keep their costs down, and families sharing not only the kitchen but also close-up care of kin.

In Sharon Astyk's book, *Depletion and Abundance—Life on the New Home Front*, she makes the point that when people change houses every few years, they end up spending lots of extra money and time settling back in, renovating things, 'getting it right', money and time that they could have spent becoming a valued member of their community.

She also discusses the idea of stewardship of the family property for future generations, something that rarely happens these days in the lives of middle-class westerners. It's more likely that our parents will sell their house to go schmoozing the world rather than actively help their grandchildren with their shelter requirements. I'm not talking about making our kids trust-fund babies (in our home, there will always be more trust than funds!), but I feel within myself a growing desire to ensure that my own children are looked out for—not looked after—in the world of their future, where prosperity and poverty may become even more marked.

I want to plant trees for them today that will feed them and their neighbours tomorrow. I want to be able to pass down to them a property that they and their own families can share if needed. My hope is that my children will be the recipients of a bountiful and carefully thought-out legacy of love; that's what my husband and I are working on (and planting!) now. Sure, they may reject it all for a life on the fiftieth floor, but at least they'll have the option, and awareness of alternative lifestyles.

I think many in our parents' generation have been as easily manipulated by the advertising industry and big business as we have. Just as we've been bombarded with 'If you drive this car, the chicks will be yours' and 'We want to help you, so here's another $5,000 on your credit card', all those Baby Boomers have been told, for profit's sake, 'You've done your bit for the kids, now it's time for you.' Of course, the advertisers conveniently left off the bit that said, 'But you're still the parent, the custodian, the elder; you still have responsibilities to future generations to ensure the planet is left in a better state than when you arrived!' In the coming years though, families may need to stay together longer and be stronger, forging bonds between us that are resistant to all the glittering 'rewards' dangled before our eyes.

I had a wonderful lesson about family early in life. It was when my great-grandfather Pa came to live with us. My dad had three sisters, so each side of the family got to look after Pa for three months at a time. He was a fantastic old guy, tall and stick-thin. When we children were up to mischief, he'd look at us with a wicked grin, and then he'd wink and say, "See no evil, hear no evil, speak no evil." We always knew he wouldn't tell on us.

Rather than placing an unbearable burden on our family, having Pa at our place was always something that we looked forward to. Sure, he used to hurl his walking stick at my dog when she stole his ginger chocolates, and we did have to put plastic wrap over the salt shaker at his end of the table because he'd forget he'd already used it and would re-salt his meal about 20 times a minute, but looking after Pa was a special part of my childhood.

Today when I was giving my own son a piggyback, I asked him when I was old would he give me a piggyback, and he said, "Of course," then he thought for a minute: "...as long as you're toilet-trained!"

Nowadays, the media harps on about the terrible burden on families who are looking after their elderly parents while raising their own kids at the same time, as if 'having it all' means having a job and a bit of time for family, so long as you don't have to invest too much time or money on the latter. It's as though family is a hassle, an interruption in the cogs of the economic machine, one that becomes a terrible struggle.

This is why we really need to question the system to which we're all slaves, because a person shouldn't be torn between jobs, a mortgage, ailing parents and school-age children. There's something inherently and odiously wrong with such a system. By getting our vocation, location, mortgage, family and housing right, it can all be made a lot easier. By questioning marketing messages that promote hyper-individualism and scoff at the thought of three generations living together, we might save ourselves a whole lot of money while gaining a whole treasure chest of memorable, invaluable moments.

If you see a future for your current location and home, that's wonderful. If this chapter has made you question things, either attend to matters and fix them, or find a place now that you will be happy to call home 20, 30, 50 years from now. Don't rush into it, though. Do thorough research. Find an area, and then a property within that area, that you would like your children and their children to grow up in. Make history together. Seek shelter and community and find somewhere that will be able to feed not only your stomach, but your spirit and soul too.

Be a family, and create that interconnected, protected, nourishing honeycomb environment where you and your children can feel safe and happy, and flourish. It might be where you are right now!

THOUGHT LAUNCHERS & CONVERSATION STARTERS

- Ask your children to name some **unsafe places to live**: "on the side of a volcano" should get the conversation started!
- Have the kids do a **natural history project** on your local area, look through old newspapers and visit the historical society to find out more about the land you're living on.
- Speak with your children about the positives and negatives of large houses, apartments, townhouses and acreages as a main **place of residence**.
- Pull out a **map** of your country (or the world for that matter!) and ask your children which five places they think would be best if they couldn't continue to live where they're living now.
- Start talking with your children about how life would look if you all still lived **together** when they were grown-ups. What would the pros and cons be? What family rules would have

to be modified? e.g., more privacy for everyone, sharing of responsibilities, etc.

- Think about your own situation. Would it be possible or desirable for you and 'the grandparents' to combine resources to purchase a more **suitable dwelling** where you could all live together?

- Ask your children what they like and dislike about **where you live now.**

- Do an **audit** of your current home to see how secure, energy efficient and productive it is. Think about the little things you can do to increase its value in these areas, such as adding water tanks to catch roof run-off, building a storage area for food, and improving the insulation.

- Ask the kids, "If we didn't have a car, or petrol was too expensive for us to fill the tank, where would be a more **convenient place** for us to live so we could still get around easily?" e.g., within reach of the ocean, a train line, a river, near a city cycleway, etc.

- Organise a week-long holiday **house swap** with a family from another city or town so you can get a feel for a different area.

Chapter 11

·······························

MONEY CAN'T BUY YOU LOVE

To be satisfied with a little, is the greatest wisdom; and he that increaseth his riches, increaseth his cares; but a contented mind is a hidden treasure, and trouble findeth it not.

AKHENATON

I fear our grandchildren will not care very much about whether in the early 21st century we sustained 20th century-style economic growth. They will be far more concerned, I suspect, about climate; about whether there is sufficient food and water; about the security measures and economic resources needed to cope with millions of environmental refugees.

That will require the emergence of an economy that not only takes care of both people and planet but also breaks the mold in terms of how we look at the world. We need a form of globalisation that empowers local communities and local cultures, with all their accumulated wisdom, to maintain their own environments. Enabling these things is not only our most urgent priority but it is also our greatest opportunity.

PRINCE CHARLES' ADDRESS TO OPEN THE NOBEL LAUREATES SYMPOSIUM ON CLIMATE CHANGE, LONDON, MAY 27 2009[3].

---

[3]Read the full address here: http://www.princeofwales.gov.uk/ speechesandarticles/a_speech_by_hrh_the_prince_of_wales_to_open_ the_nobel_laurea_1868821850.html

"Money won't make you happy," said Zig Ziglar, "but everybody wants to find out for themselves." That's why we think "If only I were rich, everything would be okay." That's why when we buy the item of our heart's desire, we discover that our heart soon beats for something else. That's why we see rich people living their lives so poorly.

For all its ills though, some amount of money is important, in that it helps us to obtain at least basic shelter, food, water and health, along with the security and peace of mind that this brings. We need some money somewhere along the line to be able to pay government fees, buy the land on which our apple tree will grow, and buy that potentially life-saving water filter. However, once these basic needs are covered, too much money can be more of a disaster than a delight, both for individuals and our planet.

I was listening to a talkback radio program the other week and an older caller summed up her feelings about having her superannuation in the stock market versus spending it on items that made her feel secure and prepared for the future. She'd wanted to spend several thousand dollars on a solar-powered system, a shed and some tools, but had decided to 'play it safe' and keep her retirement savings where they were. A few months later, after the Global Financial Crisis had wreaked havoc, she found that she'd lost the equivalent of the cost of what she'd wanted to buy. Pwoof! Just like that. No money. No solar power. No shed or tools. No peace of mind.

In the old days, young ladies put special items that would be useful or nice to have in a 'glory box' for when they got married. Now, some people are putting away things in their 'future box', believing that items like quality hand tools, water filters, solar ovens and the like will be worth way more than the wad of cash used to buy them.

In the future, there may be a time where knowing how to save heritage seeds and maintain healthy soil and a reliable source of potable water will be worth far more than having any amount of money in a bank account, but in the meantime, we owe it to our children to teach them about the world of finance.

Obviously, the notes and coins that signify money won't be going away any time soon, but we can do our children a favour by introducing them to other forms of 'money'; things like community exchange schemes, barter, and keeping an eye out for unwanted goods. Even if it's as simple as swapping fresh basil and berries for an hour of lawn-mowing, or picking up items at roadside clean-ups, try to make the connection for your children that trade without credit cards and cash is not only possible, but often preferable. Can you remember the delight of going to the garbage dump with your dad and coming home the proud owner of a doll, a scooter or some books, even if they were a little the worse for wear? Alas, for many kids today, their parents wouldn't be seen dead at the kerb, let alone the tip shop!

Of course, you can argue that without lots of cash, you can't buy any assets to start with, but that's a furphy. Just today, I visited a friend who showed me a massive shelving system in her shed. She hadn't needed thousands of dollars to purchase the set-up; all she'd done was find the courage to walk into a big-name store that was refurbishing and ask the owner if she could have their old stuff!

This lady is proof that scavenging and salvaging is a great way to either increase your wealth or live on less. Many of the items on her property have been sourced from garbage dumps. What she gets for free, other people pay through the nose for. Her approach means that she's been able to save what money she has for things she can't find through scavenging. Scavenging also provides her with tradeable stepping stones, as she swaps the items she doesn't need for ones she does.

Scavenging is a commendable environmental pursuit too, because you're recycling other people's waste, rather than generating more. So next time there's a clean-up in your area, grab the kids and head roadside for some freebies you can put to good use! It sure is an economical way to shop.

What's an economy for anyway? In David Suzuki's inspiring book, *The Sacred Balance*, he writes:

"At this critical juncture in our history on Earth, we are asking the wrong questions. Instead of 'How do we reduce the deficit?', or 'How do we carve out a niche in the global economy?', we should be asking, 'What is an economy for?', and 'How much is enough?'"

And as John Ralston Saul states in his book, *The Collapse of Globalism and the Reinvention of the World*, "For some it seems as if the moving of goods across borders was the purpose of civilisation." He also says:

"Note how many of the world's leading modern economic historians equate consumerism not with wealth creation and societal growth, but with inflation and the decline of citizenship. Why? Because there is a constant surplus of goods that relate neither to structural investment nor to a concept of economic value, let alone to societal value."

I like this quote, because it challenges me to think about many of the things I've spent money on in the past, and the complete lack of good these products have really brought my family, or civilisation, for that matter! I now have a quick think before making any purchase based on how it relates to structural investment or societal value. Buying a good-quality hand tool or homemade scarf tends to rate a whole lot higher than buying a new perfume or pair of heels!

And remember, what adds to our happiness in the moment can detract from it later. Think about how much time you spend maintaining, cleaning, fixing, storing, moving, organising, protecting and insuring all the things you own. Being free of clutter makes me think of diving into the ocean wearing just my swimmers versus taking a swim wrapped in a blanket and chains. It's the same for bees; they don't tolerate any clutter in their hives or bring in anything useless, and they remove debris as quick as they can. They know it's important for the hive's health and it works, so why don't we do the same?

One of the other most valuable lessons for children to learn about money involves exposing them to the idea of sharing. Yes, grown-ups can share too you know!

For example, why does every family in a suburban street need their own lawnmower? What an absolute waste of the world's resources, and of money. Why does every small farm need their own tractor, or horse float, or trailer?

Why does every house have to have a trampoline, Wii or soccer net, when neighbours and communities could get together to set up toy libraries, rotating items every few months, thereby giving everyone a whole range of new and fun experiences?

By giving up a tiny amount of control and being flexible, families and the environment can save a veritable fortune. That's because not only is the initial price shared, but so are the ongoing maintenance costs. By sharing with other people, it becomes possible to afford more durable and better-made items. By sharing, we decrease the amount of resources consumed through production.

Some might think that being able to own something by yourself is a sign of success, but what is success? Is success a couple with a high net worth who both hold highly paid full-time jobs that have allowed them to take on a lot of debt, buy a big house, own matching fancy cars and even a small runabout for the nanny?

Or could success be a couple with a lot lower net worth who both work part-time, grow their own food, live in a small shed while they build a modest house, and get to help out a few mornings a week at their children's school?

Success doesn't really have anything to do with money, or what you spend it on; it has to do with how fulfilled you are, and how happy you make others. It's the same for your children.

Perhaps your child sees a new car on the street and says, "That's so cool. I want one of them when I grow up." That gives you a great opportunity to fill them in on the story behind the shiny, souped-up sedan, and expand their worldview in the process.

For example, after exploring why your child thinks the car is so 'cool', you might ask one of the following questions:

- Do you think you'd be happier if we had an expensive new car?
- In what ways would you be happier? For example, because it's nice to look at, would it make you feel good?
- Do you think it would still make you feel happy two years after we bought it, when it was older?
- What things would we need to sacrifice to buy that new car? For example, we'd need to spend more hours at work, which would mean less time with you, or we'd need to move to a smaller house, or we couldn't take a holiday, etc.
- So on balance, do you think that new car would make us happier or not?
- What else might we spend the money on instead of a new car?
- Why should we spend any extra money at all?

Just by probing a little, you'll be helping your children to challenge a lot of assumptions about money and success, so hopefully they won't fall into the same traps themselves.

Ever since they earned their first dollar, we've explained to our children how important it is for them to pay themselves before they pay the shopkeeper. Let's say they want a new book that can't be borrowed from the local library, and it costs $10. The 'pay yourself first' rule means they need to save $20: $10 for their own bank account, and then $10 for the book.

It's amazing how fast your children's bank accounts swell once they get into the habit of paying themselves first. It also slows down their spending, as it takes longer for them to earn the higher amount needed. What we've also noticed is that during the extended time it takes the kids to save the extra money, they often realise that they no longer 'desperately need' the item anyway. So often, I've seen something in a shop, wanted it badly, and then continued on because of lack of time or money, only to find the next day that I didn't really need it at all.

Paying yourself first is a simple instruction that will become a habit that will help future-proof your children financially. I only wish I'd started as a child and developed the same discipline! Instead, my husband and I got way over our heads in debt, and had to fight incredibly hard to reduce it. We were lucky, but I've never forgotten the stomach-churning feeling of not having any money left just one day after pay day.

Teaching our kids how to earn a living is equally important, and it's great for them to understand that there's more than one way they can do that. They can:

- Come up with interesting business ideas and sell things to people
- Work for other people
- Create unique items for sale
- Fix things for people
- Offer services that people need
- Buy something that makes more money, e.g. buy a bucket and sponge so they can clean neighbours' cars, or buy a horse, and when it foals, sell the foal
- Buy something and then rent it to people (e.g. , toys, houses)
- Entertain people
- Put their money in a bank, which will pay them interest, or buy shares in companies that will pay them dividends (encourage them to research their choices when selecting who to bank with and what kind of investments are 'better' than others in the bigger picture).

Get them started early so they can discover how supply and demand works, and so they can begin building a nest egg and knowledge.

On the weekend, our family had a stall at a local Shakespeare Festival selling our farm-made balms and soaps. Our daughter set herself up at the end of the table with a little sign saying "Poetry on Demand". Generous teenagers and grown-ups encouraged her initiative and she made a good amount of money selling sonnets, limericks and haiku! Not bad for a ten-year-old.

When our kids earn money, it's time for them to learn how to save, spend and use it. Perhaps they could divide it five ways, enabling them to spend some, save some and share some. For example, you could suggest that they:

- Put some in the bank to buy assets that will enable them to make money in the long term without having to work
- Put some in the bank to save to buy their own home or farm
- Put some in the bank to save for a medium-term goal, e.g. something expensive that takes more than a few weeks to save for
- Have fun spending some that week, e.g. at the general store
- Donate some to charity, buy gifts for others or use the money to fund good deeds.

Having money in the bank or gold in your safe might give you a sense of security, and it might give you the power to generate even more money, or buy the things you need to secure your future, but it needs to be kept in perspective. In the future it's quite possible that value will be more about owning useful assets and skills, knowledge and land than about having a truckload of cash or share certificates.

THOUGHT LAUNCHERS & CONVERSATION STARTERS

- Your child is begging for a new expensive toy or tool. You're actually happy for them to have it, but ask them to think about someone else they know who might like to be a **part-owner**. Work out how the sharing would work, e.g. each child would have the item for one week or one month at a time. Then approach the parents of the other child to see if they would be interested in going halves in the item. What a great way to teach your child about the benefits of sharing and co-ownership. What a great way to save money and the world's resources at the same time.

- Ask your children to come up with some **jobs** they can do around the house (that you actually want done!) to earn extra money.

- Embrace the whole idea of '**not new**'. Try finding products via eBay, community notice boards and Internet sites like Craigslist, Gumtree and charity shops.

- Have your children investigate some charities they would like to support, and help them to set up a **charitable goal**.

- See if your children are interested in making something small for sale so they can begin **learning about earning**, sticking with a task, being creative and dealing with customers. They might paint recycled garden pots, or harvest and sell worm fertiliser from their own worm farm, or become a weed-picking, car-washing, card-making mogul, and learn a lot about responsibility, commitment and cash.

- **Get rid of temptation.** Keep coins in your kids' money boxes by keeping advertising catalogues and magazines away from them. Send all the guff straight to the recycling bin or put a notice on your letterbox saying junk mail is not welcome. Mute the TV during ad breaks.

- If your parents or in-laws lavish your children with gifts, ask them to choose **thoughtful gifts** that will last or gifts that will impact in a positive, long-term way: cash for a bank account, or funding of courses and activities, or a visit to a museum might be more useful and affect the environment less than electronic gadgets, plastic toys and stuffed animals. Encourage them to give your children experiences rather than things.

- Give the kids a certain amount of money and let them go wild at an **op shop or charity store**, then take them to a regular shop and work out what they would have had to spend to buy the equivalent goods (also talk about the environmental savings of buying pre-loved over new).

- Involve the kids at a carboot sale or **community market** where they can learn about value, sales, haggling and how not to spend all the profits!

- Ensure that not all your wealth is reliant on **computerised systems**. Keep printed records and investigate keeping safety deposit boxes, a small stash of cash, and putting some of your wealth into truly usable items.

- Choose not to over-consume or **waste** anything, including food, fuel, furniture, water and gadgets.

- Together, contemplate what your family really needs to spend money on to be **truly content**.

- Play a game with the kids where they write down the 10 most **important items** they think are in the house. See how many are electrical, then ask them what they think are the 10 most valuable non-electrical items. Teach them to appreciate the truly valuable items to their lives, which might be as simple as a roll of string and a sharp knife, not the wide TV screen!

- The **'Slow Money'** movement asks people to contemplate what life would be like if we were more interested in making a living than making a killing. Slow Money is about 'nurture capital' rather than venture capital. One way to get involved in Slow Money is to try to invest more of your money in your local community and/or with small farming enterprises within 50 miles of your home. Read more at www.slowmoneyalliance.org.

- Watch the 20-minute film *The Story of Stuff* with your children at www.storyofstuff.com. This short film graphically illustrates the broader costs of manufactured items.

Chapter 12

....

NATURE KNOWS BEST

Look deep into nature, and then you will understand everything better.

ALBERT EINSTEIN

Every creature is better alive than dead, men and moose and pine trees, and he who understands it aright will rather preserve its life than destroy it.

HENRY DAVID THOREAU

Nature and humanity are interconnected, but we spend most of our time avoiding nature, driving through it, closing our doors to it, ignoring it, spraying it and probably even running from it!

Richard Louv, author of *Last Child in the Woods*, has even coined a term for it: 'Nature Deficit Disorder' (NDD). It's a cute term that sums up a generation that prefers to be inside with power points rather than outside with pine trees.

If you don't want your children to suffer from NDD, find ways to get them to spend more time in nature observing it, learning from it, playing in it, and developing a connection with it.

We're all interconnected cells within nature's large honeycomb; it can't be healthy to live life cut off from nature. Sure, it might seem hard to commune with nature when you live in the city, but a short walk down your street should at least bring you to a park or a big tree, a puddle or a planter box. There are zoos, city farms and botanical gardens bursting with smells, colours and creatures. Holidays in the country rather than at resorts help expose children to the elements, animals and the environment. Allowing kids to get muddy, dirty and wet certainly means an extra load of washing, but it can bring them a whole lot of joy and counteract the sterility they face as couch potatoes. That would be novel...growing potatoes rather than being potatoes!

Many of us forget to look at the real stars at night because we're curled up inside watching the starlets instead. Many of us grab a can of toxic chemicals and spray wildly rather than gently help a spider outdoors where it would much prefer to be. Many of us feel more at home behind car doors than in the great outdoors. But many of us want something different for our children.

Wouldn't it be great if our kids were as comfortable walking in the rain as they were walking around a shopping mall? Wouldn't it be great if our kids showed the same joy at seeing a native bird as they do at seeing a fast-food logo? Wouldn't it be great if our kids felt as at ease in a forest as they do on a mown football field? Well, they can!

It's hard for an adult to overcome an aversion they've held since childhood, but it's easy to teach a child to become more comfortable in the outdoors. After all, they call it the 'great' outdoors, not the 'gross' outdoors, for a reason!

My sister likes to say, "My idea of camping is turning up to a five-star hotel without a reservation." This cracks me up, but, like her, I'm not particularly fond of camping! I'm a light sleeper, and find the noises of the night too loud to lull me into La La Land, but I'll still hoist a tent in the backyard every now and then so the kids can get a feel for something other than four walls.

Try to incorporate a love of and respect for nature whenever you can. Perhaps for your child's next birthday, instead of lashing out on toys, try 'adopting' a wild animal through a charity. From tigers to turtles, there are charities all over the world dedicated to making the lives of endangered species a little less precarious. Your children can get involved.

There's a piece of writing, said to be by American Indian Chief Seattle, who in 1854 made a profound and beautiful statement on the environment that has resonated with me since I was a teenager, and I hope it will catch my own children's hearts (the letter hangs on a wall in our house, so hopefully they'll pay attention to it one day!). It's too long to reprint here, but one of my favourite paragraphs is this:

"Teach your children what we have taught our children, that the earth is our mother. Whatever befalls the earth befalls the sons of the earth. If men spit upon the ground, they spit upon themselves. This we know, the earth does not belong to man, man belongs to earth. All things are connected."

Show your children how you care about the environment by recycling, by choosing organic over toxic, and by treading lightly rather than treading heavily and indiscriminately all over! Plan your car trips so that none are unnecessary. Buy less rather than more. Take a fair share rather than a full share.

Help your children to understand where things come from so they can make their own decisions about what they think is fair. Children should know that nuggets were once feathered chickens, that if they own a dog or a cat, many other animals have probably been put to death to feed it. That using only one side of a sheet of paper doubles the number of trees that must be cut down.

Your children need to feel comfortable being soaked by the rain, warmed by the sun and refreshed by the breeze. They can't gain respect for something they've never seen, smelt, touched or felt. Sure, they might know what a comfy couch feels like and want to sit on it day in day out, but years from now, they might be more content if they're less in tune with the stereo and more in tune with the universe.

Nature doesn't come with a remote control. You can't press a button and make nature happen. Your children need to learn to cohabit with the natural world, to move in and around the honeycomb, not control or destroy it.

Nature isn't available on the stock exchange, although some would have you believe otherwise! Try encouraging exploration of the natural environment, rather than exploitation of it. There are many opportunities to show children the difference between exploration and exploitation; it can be as simple as showing them the right way to treat pets, or encouraging them to play with shells on the beach but not allowing them to take them home. Help your children, like bees in a beehive, to be caretakers of the environment, rather than profit-makers from it.

When I look back on my city childhood, some of the strongest memories I have are of trips to the country, or time at the beach, or exploring in forests, but what memories are our children accumulating now? Will they be memories of discovery, creativity, exploration and imagination, or of remote controls, structured sports, texting, computer games and the back of our heads as we drive them places?

The other day, our son took one of our farmstay guests' children down to the dam for a spot of fishing. They trooped off with rods and buckets and a whopping big knife. I admit I was a bit nervous about the carving knife, but was determined to leave the boys alone for an hour. Just as nerves started to get the better of us parents, the kids emerged victorious with two fish for dinner and all limbs and digits intact. Allowing our kids to head into nature to test themselves is much more empowering than allowing them to choose what they want from a fast-food menu.

Our kids can gain so much from getting outdoors; we just need to encourage them to step outside. They **will** follow us, you know.

THOUGHT LAUNCHERS & CONVERSATION STARTERS

- Ask your children to write down their 10 **favourite animals** and their 10 **favourite plants**.
- As a gift, **'adopt' an endangered animal,** or plant a tree on behalf of your children.
- Think about all the 'natural' things you're uncomfortable with (spiders, rain, etc.) and consciously decide not to pass those same **aversions** on to your children.
- **Plan a holiday** with your children that's either on a farm or in a forest or wilderness area.
- If you have a backyard, think about getting some **chickens** so your children can learn to be responsible pet owners, or a worm farm to improve your garden and soak up your scraps.
- **Listen to your body**—how does your body really feel after an hour in a park compared with an hour in a shopping centre? And how long does that feeling last? There's energy in nature that no amount of artificial lighting, piped music and shiny mirrors can re-create.
- **Visit an observatory** one night with your children to give them an idea of the scope of the universe.
- Join a local group to help **rehabilitate a park** or urban area.
- **Swap your insect spray** for a flyswat or spider catcher, or just learn to put up with them.
- Have the kids look in your local street directory to find a nearby bushland area that they haven't been to before. Hike, cycle or drive to it and **spend the morning exploring** and just being out and about.

- Take a train ride to an outer urban area and go exploring for the day. **Carry all you need** in backpacks and bring any rubbish home.
- Do some **'guerrilla gardening'** with your kids in which you plant useful seeds and plants in poorly used spaces.
- Empty your garbage bin out at the end of the week and see what makes up the bulk of your **household waste.** Ask the children for ideas on how to cut down on the worst of it.
- Loan the kids your digital camera and have them take **pictures of nature** in your backyard or from your balcony.
- Set up a nature **scavenger hunt** in which the kids need to locate different types of leaves, scat (animal poo!) and other items in your backyard or street.
- **Set up a tent** in the backyard for the weekend, and actually sleep in it! Or let them lie out on the grass until they fall asleep, only bringing them inside if you have to.
- **Serve morning tea, lunch and dinner outside** more often.
- **Lie on a picnic blanket,** look up at the bigger picture, and tell stories about the clouds.

Chapter 13

....

LAUGHTER IS THE BEST MEDICINE

Cynicism is humour in ill health.

H. G. WELLS

Against the assault of laughter—nothing stands.

MARK TWAIN

*At the height of laughter, the universe is flung
into a kaleidoscope of new possibilities.*

JEAN HOUSTON

Having a sense of humour is like carrying a cure-all
everywhere you go. It gives us a way of relieving
our distress and heightening our happiness. Laughter helps us to
cope, and to make sense of this crazy world. Just the simple act of
smiling seems to have an effect on even the blackest mood.

Being able to laugh when we trip up, chuckle when we embarrass
ourselves, and smile when we're faced with the day-to-day grind
takes the sting out of our lows and heightens our highs.

Our kids really need to understand the philosophy that although we can't control what happens to us, we can control how we react. Showing them you can react with humour to most situations is a gift that will help them be light-hearted rather than heavy-hearted.

The other day, I had to practice what I preach. I was taking a farm guest out to show them the hives, and we'd walked about 500 metres in our beekeeping overalls before popping our hoods on. We spent about 30 minutes going through three hives, carefully checking for disease, swapping frames and cutting the grass in front of the landing areas so the bees didn't have to dodge tall grass stalks. I was feeling and sounding confident and knowledgeable, and was bent over holding a full frame of bees from the fourth hive when I felt something move near my scalp, then across my ear, and then across my face. Holy beeswax! A mouse was in my hood, eyeballing me! Being an allergic-to-bees beekeeper, I couldn't rip the hood off to let the mouse escape because I had an open box of bees in front of me and bees flying all around. It was awful. I was trapped in a hood with a mouse doing laps of my face! The guest—who I had been trying to impress—was staring at the mouse and me, horrified. I was mortified. It was completely and utterly gross. Completely out of my control. Awful. But it was hilarious! I just made sure I laughed with my mouth shut (and yes, with a bit of help, the mouse finally escaped across my face, over my ear, down my neck, across my back, up my shoulder, via my armpit, and out my sleeve).

There are so many moments every day where we're given the opportunity to show our children how to react with fun rather than frustration, with giggles rather than glares, moments of tension that, with a humorous twist or a less combative approach, can leave us laughing rather than licking our wounds. From spilt milk to messy rooms, selfish drivers to slow supermarket aisles, each is an opportunity for us to show our children how humour or even a gentle smile can heal instead of harden.

We recently went on a family holiday, and within an hour of setting out our youngest vomited all over herself—and her horrified brother and sister. We had to stop the car, pull everything out of the jam-packed rear to get to some fresh clothes from her suitcase, and then unpack another bag to find cloths we could use as wipes. While we were doing all this, we were attacked by mosquitoes. Squadrons of them! It was horrible, but it was hilarious. The car and seats stank, we spent the next hour swatting stowaway mozzies, and finally spent two hours at a laundromat because the smell of the vomit was just suffocating inside the car. And yet we chose to see the funny side of the incident, and laughed heartily at the 'Griswold family vacation' moment rather than kicking up (even more of) a stink. Thank goodness we did, because the next day of driving saw the other daughter vomit four times! These incidents ended up being recalled as two of the many highlights of the holiday.

Being a little crazy, being able to laugh at ourselves, being able to share joy is a way to be kinder to ourselves and others. Our children will benefit from experiencing less angst. They'll learn that sadness can be tinged with happiness, that although life isn't always easy, it doesn't have to be a glum ride all the way to the end.

Humour can be gentle, it can be rollicking, it can be subtle, it can be stomach-bursting and it can be intensely personal, as anyone who's told a joke to a crowded room can testify. We don't all think the same things are funny! Some people tell a joke that to them is hilarious, only to find that they've offended the person they're telling it to because it comes across as crude, political, sexist or racist.

We definitely don't want our children to be amused by other people's suffering, but it's great if they can see the funny side of their own trials. We don't want our kids to laugh at others, but we do want them to be able to laugh at themselves. We don't want them to be offensive, but wouldn't it be great if they grew up to be hard to offend?!

Some kids just seem to be born with a jovial nature, while others present as sterner and more serious, but they can all benefit from seeing you interpret life's ups and downs with less frowns, more fun. Even serious talks can be lightened up with a bit of jest.

Being more casual than critical gives everyone a little extra breathing space as they face up to tough times.

Some jokes and humour are about making scapegoats, and spreading darkness and cynicism, but a good sense of humour can help relax us, lower our stress levels, give us hope, and is, well, just plain enjoyable. It makes it easier for us to meet new people, it encourages our creativity and spontaneity, and, as they say, laughter is the best medicine. Gentle humour can help ease suffering, make us stronger when we're under threat, and send rays of light into corners of gloom.

Humour can often be found just by shifting our perspective. It can give us new ways of seeing a bad situation. Having that flexibility of thought gives our children a whole array of opportunities, rather than them being bogged down by the worst-case scenario.

A sense of humour is also a great tool with which to equip your children to enhance their ability to be part of a strong community. As Dwight D Eisenhower said, "A sense of humour is the art of leadership, of getting along with people, of getting things done." In the years ahead, as cooperation becomes more important than competition, a sense of humour will be a valuable personal trait.

When we see the world too seriously, it loses some of its magic, but when we see it with a glint in our eye, we can enjoy the good with the bad, and the ridiculous with the reverential, thus making the most of our time here. Humour can distract, defuse and delight, so let's let loose with the giggles!

THOUGHT LAUNCHERS & CONVERSATION STARTERS

- The next time something bad happens to you, find a way to see it in a more **humorous** light.
- **Borrow some joke books** from your library.

- Have a '**stand-up comedy' night** at home one weekend with each child and parent telling some jokes, dressing up funny or doing something silly.
- Consciously choose to **smile rather than scowl.**
- Come up with some funny ways your children can respond to **bullies.**
- When your children are **frowning,** laugh and recite that cheesy motto, "Turn that frown upside down."
- If your child's face is set sternly, every now and then remind them in a nice way to "**relax your face.**"
- **Start smiling at things that drive you crazy,** like stop signs and traffic lights. It's weird to do, but it actually changes how you feel about the interruption.
- **Gently** help your children to see the funny side of situations they perceive as upsetting.
- Start making ordinary moments funny moments. Whether it's in the kitchen or in the car, try and **get some more giggles going!**
- Make **funny faces** instead of sour faces.

Chapter 14

A SENSE OF PERSPECTIVE

The universe is change; our life is what our thoughts make it.
MARCUS AURELIUS

Happiness is an inside job.
WILLIAM A. WARD

Perspective is all about having the ability to see what something is within a wider context. People who have perspective seem to have an ability to cope with life's swings and roundabouts thanks to their ability to deal with good times and bad. Perspective is about point of view. It's about how you see the world and the people in it.

Children who are encouraged to see how others live, who feel empathy with those who have less, and more, and who mingle with people of different race, wealth, health and point of view, may have a greater opportunity to widen their perspective than those who are mollycoddled and kept cocooned, or who are taught to compete with—rather than coexist with—other people.

Perspective isn't about facts; it's about how we process our thoughts about those facts.

We get perspective by being exposed to different ideas, different people and different environments, by experiencing different commentators, points of view, and even music!

When I started beekeeping, I spent two days in a classroom, read lots of traditional texts and watched documentaries about traditional ways of beekeeping. I began with Italian honey bees and did everything I was told, including buying queens in little cages rather than letting the bees raise their own, and I used standard hives. However, over the years, as I've been exposed to more information, different beekeepers, read other points of view and even experimented with different species of bees, I've developed a much broader perspective about why I beekeep and how I want to beekeep. There have been lots of learning curves, amazing honey flows, draining days and huge setbacks, but having some perspective has kept my commitment and enthusiasm high.

Perspective enables us to rise above minor grievances, aches and let-downs. When we don't get bogged down in the everyday disappointments of life, we're able to enjoy life more and contribute more.

It's easy to feel sorry for yourself when you can't afford the most expensive pair of runners, until you see someone without any shoes at all. It's easy to feel sorry for yourself when you sprain your ankle, until you visit a ward full of amputees. It's easy to feel sorry for yourself when your car won't start and you have to leg it to the bus stop, until you see someone walking along the side of the road who can't even afford the bus fare.

The ability to see life for what it is—a fleeting opportunity—gives us the ability to live in the moment and live well. Do we want to waste an hour feeling bitter when we'll never have that hour again? Might we choose to greet our spouse more positively each morning, knowing that it may be our last? Is it worth getting all emotional over a problem that can easily be resolved and that won't even be a blip on our radar 12 months from now?

As parents, it's our responsibility to help our children widen their perspective and embrace the bigger picture, indeed to teach them that perspective is actually a wonderful tool that they can control for themselves.

You can start by explaining that perspective can't be found by following the lives of celebrities through the pages of a magazine; that it's discovered in the real world, not in computer games; that looking out rather than looking in makes us happier in the long run. Self-absorption literally sucks the perspective right out of us.

Mix it up by exposing your children to families that don't necessarily share the same income and philosophies as yours. It may not always be smooth sailing, but it's all about broadening your children's view of the world. There's always something we can learn from others (even if that something happens to be patience!), and by blending the best of what you come across with your family's unique way of doing things, your children's perspective improves.

Gossips don't seem to have a whole lot of perspective, so encourage your children to be broad-minded rather than narrow-minded. Help them to see the grey when others only see the black or the white.

The ability to understand the motivations and actions of other human beings will be crucial to their future in so many ways. They will only learn how to do this if they look out, not in.

Let's say one of your children has had a run-in with another child at school, and has been bullied. First, provide them with a safe place and tend to their fears. Then, put them in the shoes of the bully. Ask them why they think the bully is doing what they're doing. Ask them to think about various ways of dealing with the situation, and then ask them what their backup plan is if the first one fails.

It's hard enough to understand our own selves sometimes, but we also need to help develop our children's understanding of others. They need to experience other types of people, families, cultures and communities. It's this experience that will eventually help them to understand all sides of a story.

There are daily opportunities to teach our children perspective. Here's a simple example we experienced the other night. Our youngest daughter dressed herself in some of her favourite clothes to go out to dinner with her grandparents. Though we regularly message that it's who she is, not what she wears that's important, and that we really only wear clothes to stop us being naked, cold or exposed to the sun, she does seem to take quite some pride in putting her outfits together!

Once we were all seated at the table, the waiter presented her with a large glass of orange juice and suddenly, whoops, over it went, a torrent of sticky orange liquid drenching her outfit. Dinner had just started, we were 30 minutes from home, and it was cold. We had to make do. We borrowed her brother's jacket for her top, tied her cardigan around her waist like a skirt and tried to help her get past her disappointment.

She was upset at spilling the juice, angry, embarrassed, crushed, and definitely didn't like wearing 'boy clothes'. "Everything, EVERYTHING, is ruined," she wailed.

The next few minutes were spent explaining that, actually, not 'everything' was ruined. It was just that her clothes were a bit wet, and they could easily be washed. Unfortunately, that didn't work because she was still mightily embarrassed, so after acknowledging that we understood why she was upset, we gave her a while to get over it. That didn't happen either, so next we decided to help her put it in perspective.

"Everything ruined," I said, "would have been if when the drink spilled it was actually a cup full of superglue that got stuck in your hair, and when I tried to get it out I got stuck to your hair, then when Daddy tried to get me out, he got stuck to my hair…"

I didn't need to go on. She smiled. From somewhere within that little body, she found the ability to accept what had happened and moved on.

Sometimes in the West we do so much for our children and give

160

them so much that we tend to create a vortex of "I want more, more, more!" To help develop our children's sense of balance, we need to remind them how privileged they are in that they have parents who love them, as well as food, water and shelter. Everything else is a luxury that the bulk of the world's population doesn't enjoy. If we constantly give, give, give, we have to expect that our children will continue to take, take, take. We're setting them up to be needy, insatiable, bottomless pits, and we don't need to do this.

We can help our children to refocus from being recipients to being givers. It's easy to think that everyone lives the kind of life we lead, or better, until we deliberately take a walk outside our cosy cocoons and into the real world.

In John Ralston Saul's book, *The Unconscious Civilization,* he talks about the elites in society "building a wall between themselves and reality by creating an artificial sense of wellbeing on the inside."

It's an interesting historical view. So, if you want your children to have a true rather than artificial sense of wellbeing, encourage them to help others, encourage them to help you, and find them lots of opportunities to do so!

What are some good deeds you and the kids can do during the next school holidays? Can you spend a few days on a farm working as WWOOFers (Willing Workers on Organic Farms), or can you team up with Habitat for Humanity to help build a house in your area? Is there some charitable work you can do in an isolated community in your country, or would you be willing to take your pets to the local retirement home to give the residents some enjoyment?

Henry David Thoreau wrote, "It is something to be able to paint a particular picture or carve a statue, and so to make a few objects beautiful; but it is far more glorious to carve and paint the very atmosphere and medium through which we look, which morally we can do. To affect the quality of the day, that is the highest of arts."

Perspective rules!

THOUGHT LAUNCHERS & CONVERSATION STARTERS

- Research some charities that will enable your children to **get involved** with others less fortunate than themselves.
- If your children are really **whingeing** about not getting the latest and greatest gadgets or clothes, first of all listen to their reasons as to why they want them so badly and help them pinpoint their motivations. Then work with them to see if the purchase will satisfy the motivation long term.
- When one of your children comes home from school with a story about a child who is being unkind to them, ask them to **put themselves in the shoes of the other child** and to talk about some possible reasons for their poor behaviour (e.g. maybe their parents yell at them too much at home, maybe their big brother beats up on them, maybe they just had a haircut they don't like, maybe their pet fish died, etc.).
- Ask your children to write a list of all the things they're **grateful** for.
- Encourage them to join the **debating team** at school, because debating encourages analysis, awareness, objectiveness, open-mindedness and the ability to see all sides of a scenario.
- Use **humour** to dilute or diffuse a situation where your child is struggling to see the bigger picture. Encourage a more healthy sense of perspective by showing understanding for their upset while at the same time explaining that things could be a lot worse—and definitely a lot funnier!

Chapter 15

THE FIVE R'S: REDUCE, REUSE, REPAIR, RECYCLE, REDISTRIBUTE

If a man walks in the woods for love of them half of each day, he is in danger of being regarded as a loafer. But if he spends his days as a speculator, shearing off those woods and making the earth bald before her time, he is deemed an industrious and enterprising citizen.

HENRY DAVID THOREAU

Our personal consumer choices have ecological, social, and spiritual consequences. It is time to re-examine some of our deeply held notions that underlie our lifestyles.

DAVID SUZUKI

Back in the early 1900s, Archaeologist Theodore M. Davis was a private sponsor with Egypt's Supreme Council of Antiquities. He discovered a number of tombs within the pyramids, along with a jar of 3000-year-old honey. The honey was still edible. It makes me think that if we start with an item of quality and use a quality production process, so many items we currently discard could, and should, last much more than a lifetime.

'Quality' is an important message in our children's lives. Quality items, quality relationships, quality food, quality time. If only we devoted more of our day to quality, the world would be a whole lot better off. Things would be built to last, the sea wouldn't be awash with plastic junk, our health would be better due to quality nutrition and our children would benefit from quality time. You don't necessarily get quality if you buy a 'quality' brand; you get quality when you know the source of the products you're buying and the process by which they've been made. You get quality when you match the need with the right tool. You get quality when the maker and the recipient benefit equally.

Like it or not, we have a responsibility to future generations. Like it or not, we and our children will make a difference based on the choices we make now. Like it or not, wasting resources is going to get a whole lot more expensive—to our hip pockets, our waistlines, our world.

The good news is that getting engaged in reducing, reusing, repairing, recycling and redistributing is exciting and empowering, especially when you realise that your choices DO matter! Even if you've been the world's worst waster up until now, your choice to live differently will matter as soon as you make that first move. And your children will be by your side, learning from everything you do, so when they're adults they'll be well prepared for any limitations on resources, they'll be adept at finding solutions and they'll be able to deal with scarcity.

Look, to be truly environmentally friendly, we would have to reject all mod cons, live in a very basic shelter and grow 100 per cent of our own food. That's extreme, and it's not going to wash too well with 99.9 per cent of the Western population, but there's no denying that we can all make strides to create a better balance, a more workable and prosperous honeycomb of life. Restraint doesn't have to be a negative. What is one man's weekly power consumption is another's lifetime consumption; what is one person's tin shed is another's mansion; what is one family's weekly food consumption might save an entire village from starvation. We need to do the best we can in moving to a life of less, without being ridiculous about it.

There's a wonderful term called 'stewardship', which is about being entrusted with something precious. It's about being a careful and responsible manager of that with which you have been entrusted. It's about personal responsibility. Imagine if we all committed to being stewards of the Earth's resources, our communities, our people, and our possessions. The world would be a very different place.

The key environmental messages children need to be familiar with are reduce, reuse, repair, recycle and redistribute.

REDUCE

Reducing our consumption supercharges our positive impact on the environment. It means less strain on the world's resources, it improves air quality, and it reduces negative impacts on health. A message of reduction is the best environmental message to try to give our kids, because by simply consuming less, we eliminate many of the problems we have ahead of us.

You can consume less by only buying durable items, and then by looking after the things that you have, by encouraging the kids to treat items with respect, by reinforcing the message that "This table needs to last a lifetime, so please don't walk across it in your boots!"

Luckily, it's easy to lead by example. Instead of using plastic or paper cups, take a reuseable mug when you order that next cappuccino; use fabric shopping bags, not plastic; take your lunch in a lunch box, or take a plate to the takeaway instead of walking away with more plastic containers every time. Instead of buying new clothes each season, buy only every other year and only if you really need new items. Reduce your use of water and electricity. Avoid products in excess packaging, and reduce your reliance on unnecessary items.

Small modifications like these will have a huge impact on everything from your bank balance to your waistline to landfill.

REUSE

Marketing gurus would have us believe that the only sanitary way to clean a house is with antibacterial disposable wipes. Some of us throw out leftovers rather than turning them into a tasty dish the following night. We throw away perfectly good containers that could be reused for other purposes. We use disposable razors rather than well-made ones.

The term 'disposable' has to go! Encourage your child to buy durable items only, or items that can be used on multiple occasions. If you buy honey or jam, keep the bottles and reuse them as candle-holders, or for your own produce, or as containers for gifts. Only buy items that are built for the long haul, not the trash haul.

REPAIR

I remember when, to my mother's despair, I used to throw out a skirt because a button had fallen off—mea culpa! Sometimes it seems crazy to repair something when it's so cheap to replace, but it's not cheap to replace when you add in all the environmental costs of purchasing a new product and creating more waste, so whenever you can, repair before you toss!

RECYCLE

When you can't repair, recycle everything you can. Try to choose recycled products when buying 'new' items. Salvage items that others don't want and turn them into treasures of your own. Recycling helps keep things out of landfill, uses less energy, and save loads of natural resources.

Embrace the vintage clothing trend—it may not be everyone's bag, but if you don't want to run into someone at a party with the same outfit as you, it's definitely a goer! Choose items that can be reclaimed by the earth, such as bamboo-handled toothbrushes instead of the millions of plastic ones that ultimately end up in landfill each year.

REDISTRIBUTE

When you have a surplus, share it. When you have an item you no longer need, offer it to friends or to a local charity or opportunity shop. Get rid of all the things in your house that you don't need, and help them find a home that does need them! Redistribute ideas, tips, and love, too! Re-gift the gift. Get onto eBay or help the kids set up a stall at a market and discover the real meaning of 'One person's trash is another's treasure.'

Teaching responsibility is a biggie too. I don't know about your kids, but ours still think that if they ruin something through rough handling or by leaving it out in the rain that we should replace it for them. I have to tell you, it's a long, hard road getting the message across. We've finally had to crack down, because it's the only way they're going to learn the value of items. If something becomes unusable due to their mishandling, either through neglecting to store it out of the rain or sun, or by breaking it in an angry outburst, it's gone. No replacement. End of story.

The Global Financial Crisis has brought with it some semblance of a return to frugality. The GFC has actually given many of us just the excuse we needed to jump off the roundabout of endless consumption. It's given us some backup in our explanations to the kids as to why they can't have the latest gadget, scooter or fashion item!

Next time you or your children really do need an item, don't just head off to the shops or buy it online. Ask the kids to think if they or someone they know might be able to make it, or go to an op shop, or visit your local tip to see if you can get what you need second-hand and at a super price.

When that button falls off, don't throw the whole shirt away. Invest in a small sewing kit, or cook a meal for a sew-happy neighbour in return for their services. Change the buttons and it could look like a whole new shirt!

Save on your holiday money! Rather than going on a fancy holiday, find someone in a different city to swap houses with for a week. Then all you'll have to pay for is the cost of the transport to get there. Even swapping sides of the city or just into a different suburb will give you a chance to get away from the day-to-day routines and explore and experience new things…at a fraction of the cost of a 'real' holiday.

Finally, scrutinise a product closely before you decide to buy, because what you find out might turn you completely off the purchase, for example the mobile phones that give off potentially damaging radiation, the cosmetics that poison, the synthetically fragrant candles with their beautiful but toxic scents.

THOUGHT LAUNCHERS & CONVERSATION STARTERS

- Think about ways in which you can **simplify** your family's life, and therefore reduce your consumption of resources.
- Replace disposable items in your home with **good-quality reusable** ones such as cloth napkins. Use good lunch boxes instead of plastic wrap.
- Before you buy a new high-cost but low-use item, such as a ladder, canvas the neighbourhood in case someone already has one or would like to **share the purchase** with you.
- Visit your local garbage dump or opportunity shop to buy **pre-loved items.**
- Learn how to maintain and repair a **bicycle**, and start using it!
- Try to stop using plastic bags for your garbage. Instead, do what our elders did: **wrap your garbage in old newspapers.**

- Explain the idea of **stewardship** to your children. Give them something they can be personally responsible for and encourage their efforts, acknowledge their care.
- There are some fantastic **books** out there with all sorts of tips about how to cut down on your energy use and how you can positively impact the environment, so borrow them from the library and share them with friends.
- The next time one of your children has a birthday party, discuss the option of putting on the invitation that **presents aren't necessary,** but if people would like to make a gesture, they could gift something that is pre-loved or locally made or some cash that could go toward a long-term saving goal.
- Think deeply with your family about the call from some quarters for an increase in **nuclear power stations.** A safer option might be to reduce our reliance on all forms of power, rather than creating more capacity that will create a new set of problems in the future.
- Have the children research what **wind-up items** they can substitute for electric or battery-operated ones.
- **Don't flick on the airconditioner or central heating** at the first "I'm cold/I'm hot" whinge. Have the kids put another layer of clothing on, or strip one off.
- Sign your kids up for the **DIY and repair courses** held by hardware stores and mechanics.
- Get involved with a local **toy-repair charity** so you and the kids can learn useful skills while also helping others.
- Start **lobbying lawmakers** and authorities about changes to laws that encourage wastefulness; there are so many of them out there! For example, why can't a small farm sell honey in a sparkling clean but previously used glass jar to a customer who knows and wants what they're getting?
- Investigate **joining** Cubs, Scouts, Brownie or Guide groups who are known for being big on craftsmanship, social responsibility and sense of community.

- Designate one day a month as a **'power party'** where you turn the power off completely for 24 hours. Turn the whole concept of no electricity into an adventure for your children. Ask them how they think they could cook your meals and keep items in the fridge cold. Work out how to bathe without electrically heated water, how you'll get around in the dark, and how you'll entertain yourselves with no electronic gadgets, TV or stereo. And now for the even more enjoyable part: work out what you'll do with all the money you'll save by reducing your annual power consumption!

Chapter 16
....
COMPASSIONATE CONSUMPTION

Advertising is the art of convincing people to spend money they don't have for something they don't need.

WILL ROGERS

Advertising: the science of arresting the human intelligence long enough to get money from it.

STEPHEN LEACOCK

We've all been there haven't we? Felt the thrill of being able to choose something of our own. Desired the dangled carrot, bought stuff to fit in, fill up, be fashionable. That's because the urge to own the latest and greatest is like a drug, because we're the targets of unrelenting commercial pressure, and after all, isn't 'out with the old and in with the new' the mantra we've grown up with?

A few years ago, I was out strolling with friends on a sunny day when suddenly someone's child pointed excitedly skyward. High above our heads, a plane looped-the-loop, writing the name of a major sunglasses brand in smoke.

Watching the cloud-like letters take shape brought back the same sense of amazement I'd felt as a child, but our then six-year-old soon brought us all back to earth. "It's just marketing you know. They're just trying to sell us stuff."

One of my friends looked horrified at my daughter's take on the aerobatics, seeing her comment as a lack of innocence, rather than the way I saw it: a lack of gullibility coupled with awareness of the world around her. No matter how jarring her statement, my daughter was technically correct. She'd hit on the fact that although it was thrilling to watch the plane looping about, and intriguing to decipher the letters, at its heart it was just an unnecessary, polluting advertisement on a big, blue billboard. Worse, it was corporate graffiti in a public space, an invasion of our day.

I breathed a sigh of relief. My daughter seemed to have absorbed the message about the insidious world of marketing. Unfortunately, not a minute had passed before she turned her eyes from the sky to a food wrapper lying in the gutter. "Can we go to McDonald's today, Mum?"

And that sums it up for me. The power and scope of marketing, the pull of temptation and how damn hard it is to be ecologically and future focused when we're force-fed by professional marketers every day.

In a health shop the other day my son pointed excitedly at boxes with a big label touting Manuka Honey Moisturising Cream. I was excited too, until I read the ingredients and discovered that the honey was about the 12th ingredient after a pile of synthetic ones.

It's not an easy thing to admit to being duped, but that's what's happening to us, our friends, our neighbours, our leaders, our doctors, our teachers and our kids. I don't know about you, but over my lifetime, I've bought truckloads of items—often on the spur of the moment. I've salivated over luxuries, saved for 'must-haves', bought on a high only to feel the low a month later when the credit card statement arrived. I cringe at the thought of how many things

I've bought and then thrown out after just one use, one season, or maybe one year. We've all done it, haven't we?

It's not fair to set our kids up for a future where they'll be slaves to unfulfilling careers, bosses and banks just so they can buy things they don't really need (and that the whole world will have to chip in to dispose of!). It's not helpful for them to waste their hard-earned money on stuff that will only make them happy momentarily.

By educating our children to base their purchases on facts rather than marketing manipulation, we'll teach them that they're not missing out when they keep their cards and cash in their pockets, rather than buying the latest bling and gadgets. They'll learn that 'things' don't fix holes in souls, that "If only I had X, I'd be happy" is just what the corporations want them to think.

It's sad that our community encourages our children to be 'consumers' rather than 'citizens', that our society asks for cash from our kids, rather than any real personal contribution. It must leave our children feeling hollow, because where once they were needed in the family unit and community to help with important tasks, now our society only encourages them to help themselves.

For kids to be able to hold out against marketing temptation more often than they give in, they need an understanding of how the marketing industry works. And work it does—brilliantly.

Northrop Frye, a Canadian literary critic, once called advertising "a judicious mixture of flattery and threats." How right he was. Marketing is a magnificent maelstrom of art and science. It involves creative exploitation of our fears, greed, ignorance and insecurities, and they even create new ones we never even knew we had before! It relies on our lack of time, lack of self-control and lack of focus on what really matters. It relies on our willingness to buy the sizzle, not the steak.

Kids can't comprehend that corporations pay millions of dollars to researchers to work out ways to get people to buy, that merchandising experts organise music and lighting to ensure we take home more than we planned, that supermarkets have super-sized trolleys because it's human nature to want to fill them up. Even we adults ignore the fact that professionals are paid six-figure sums to learn about and then exploit our vices, desires, fears and trigger points.

Kids have trouble fully digesting that it's cold, hard economic calculation and manipulation behind those soft, warm, fun, exciting, evocative and provocative marketing messages that we're bombarded with via TV, the Internet, magazines, movies, songs, electronic games, billboards, T-shirts, mascots, freebies and celebrity spokespeople.

The marketing industry is incredibly active in setting trends, as well as exploiting grassroots ones. Recently, it's been really interesting to watch corporations reacting and responding to the new wave of ethical and environmentally aware citizens. At first, they were probably frightened by the thought of their customers downshifting and seeking a simpler life, but they've quickly adapted, jumping on the bandwagon, positioning themselves as enablers of 'the new you'.

Ah, there's a return to home cooking and an interest in slow cookers, here's a packet of spices and pre-cubed meat to make it easier! Ah, people are beginning to care more about the environment, let's do what we should have done all along, make our product more concentrated so we can package it in a smaller box and claim it's better for the environment (forgetting to mention that it's still full of chemicals inside!). Ah, we know our product is totally unnecessary and polluting, so we're going to put a cute picture of an orangutan on the cover, donate to a nice green rainforest cause and try to get you to forget all that other unnecessary, damaging stuff we do.

Whether it's doctors prescribing medication instead of life-changing advice, or a school stocking its canteen with junk food, or our children pestering us for a new electronic game, the advertising industry and the vendors of commercialism have a whole lot to answer for.

Advertisers love getting to kids when they're young, because they have 'pester power', they have pocket money, they have parents who don't want them to 'miss out', and one day, the kids are going to have a pay packet of their own; the perfect target!

Corporations like to set up preferences early because they know that if you grow up eating their white bread, it's going to be hard for another advertiser (or nutritionist!) to get you to shift over to a different brand, let alone wholemeal!

From the hardware store that puts on free jumping castles and face-painting in the car park, to the chain bakery that gives kids a little smiley stamp, to the bank that hands out balloons, we need to point out and explain to our kids that the companies aren't doing it because they're being nice; they're doing it to give us a positive feeling about their brand. They're doing it to help give parents a momentarily happy kid so we will stay longer and spend more, or come back sooner. They're doing it to try and snag that unquestioning young customer for life.

A side benefit to corporations having children grow up with a positive feeling for their brand is that these children will probably be less likely to question the business's operations at a later date. For example, how could anyone not like a national chain store that regularly offers free face-painting for kids and the cheapest prices around? Well, maybe they don't pay their staff a living wage or treat them with respect. Perhaps the factories that produce their products are high polluters. Maybe the presence of such a big store crushes small local competitors, which leads to less diversity and, over time, higher prices. Maybe that free face-painting isn't so free after all.

We need to share these same ideas with our kids so they become more than puppets having their purse strings pulled by the brightest minds in the creative world.

Teenagers are savvier than younger kids, but researchers know their hot buttons inside out. Teens want to fit in, they feel pressured to conform, they want to communicate, and they want to be cool.

Teens can easily convince themselves that they're doing the choosing, even though they're still 'choosing' from brands specifically set up to target them.

Pre-teens and teens are constantly manipulated by advertisers who make use of celebrities to wear and promote their products. They're manipulated through messaging that plays on their fears of social rejection. They're manipulated by companies planting undercover marketers on social networking sites, and they're even manipulated by other trendsetting teens who are sucked into the marketing hype early. These 'Trojan Teens', as I like to call them, are the trendsetters who pack a wallop in the fight for your kids' wallets. You've heard the saying, and might have even said it to your parents when you were growing up, "But all my friends have one!"—you can thank Trojan Teens (and their parents!) for that.

Here are 10 reasons (plus a free bonus reason!) why irresponsible marketing has a negative impact on your children and the world at large (and why you should give a damn):

1. It encourages consumption of unnecessary goods. This leads to depletion of non-renewable resources and an increase in pollution.
2. It focuses us outward rather than inward for our sense of wellbeing.
3. It creates a sense of need where there wasn't one before.
4. It crushes competition...the bigger the company, the bigger the marketing budget—and therefore the harder it is for small businesses to compete.
5. Marketers often play upon our worst fears and vanities, making unimportant things seem important, creating jealousy and dissatisfaction where none previously existed.
6. It distracts us from the really important issues.
7. Companies with big name-brand products have the profits and clout to employ some of society's brightest minds, thus taking them away from other sectors of the community

where their skills and passions could have been much more valuable to society.

8. It sucks us in while sucking our savings out of our accounts. We'll never get that money back!

9. It targets our young, well before they have the knowledge or skills to resist.

10. The marketing industry is huge; its tentacles reach everywhere, to everyone, at all hours of the day and night. It's so insidious that it affects everything we do.

11. It has the money and power to lobby and squeeze through any loopholes that attempt to keep it on the straight and narrow.

So, how do we extract our families from the loop? One of the quickest ways to curtail desire for stuff is to stop looking through catalogues and magazines. Just by not opening a catalogue, you won't be distracted by a desire for things you didn't know you needed until you saw them.

Mute the TV on ad breaks (it's so easy and effective), or do what some pioneering families have already done—give away the screen altogether!

Don't 'go to the shops'; go to buy groceries. Like a horse with blinkers, I try not to look in the windows as we walk to where we're going. I think that shows the kids we really are just buying groceries, not 'shopping'. They've now learnt from many grocery-buying trips that it's possible, and normal, to return without impulse purchases.

Shopping with—and sticking to—a list is the other old lifesaver. It's been a great way to put a stop to my own tendency to pick up unnecessary items, and it also curbs the kids asking for junk food and cheap toys (all conveniently placed by the shopkeepers at child height of course!). In the first few years of their lives I repeated so often, "Sorry, it's not on the list. We only get what's on the list."

And now it's finally sunk in: they might be able to argue with me, but they can't argue with the pre-prepared list.

Casual chats with children about advertising and the difference between needs and wants also helps diminish the power marketing holds over our children, as does steering them to books rather than ad-laden magazines. It's hard to say "no" all the time, but don't become an enabler of bad habits by giving them the money for them. Enable them in positive ways instead.

Of course, as kids grow up and earn their own money, this isn't so easy. That's why we need to alert our kids to the fact that the models and celebrities we see in magazines and movies are all airbrushed, lit up, and made up to within an inch of their lives. They need to know that the portrayal of these girls and women, boys and men, is just more sleight-of-hand marketing, as advertisers try to portray an ideal that is not natural, achievable, notable or noble.

Perhaps ask your kids to think about the differences between 'appearance', 'accomplishment' and 'achievement'. What have these people actually accomplished, except perhaps having their hair done and zipping themselves in? I really love the difference between these words, 'appearance', 'achievement' and 'accomplishment'; they're words that make it so easy for children to get the concept.

Audrey Hepburn once said, "For beautiful lips, speak kind words." What another great message to give our children…that true beauty comes from what we do and say, not how we look.

When my mum turned eighty, I told her how great she still looked. Eyes bright, smile wide, she looked at me wryly: "I wouldn't know. I don't look that closely in the mirror anymore." My mum had accepted who she was and what she looked like, and was not looking to find fault with herself. What a commonsense gift to herself. By not being self-absorbed about her looks, my mum had effectively and gracefully decided that her looks mattered nowhere near as much as what she did in her life, and with whom. That's how I feel now, making choices and changes in my life. That's how I'd love my kids to feel.

As an adult, you probably know just how easy it is to feel dissatisfied after reading a women's magazine. Within the first few pages, we find that our complexion is too sallow, our hair too stringy, our kids' clothes so last season, our holiday destination passé. We feel guilty that we can't cook a Michelin Star restaurant-quality banquet and that even if we could, it wouldn't look nearly as nice on our mismatched dinner setting. Then there's the surge of jealousy when reading about the socialite who seamlessly juggles career, kids, fitness, labradoodle lap pup, opening nights and a weekly romantic picnic with her husband. Awww, shucks. Of course, she never mentions her PA, nanny, personal trainer, dog whisperer, stylist and caterer! Toward the end of the magazine, we're brimming with such pent-up desire that we fixate on the ad promoting the nearby franchise of that famous plastic surgeon. Maybe he can help fix us! If advertising can make a grown-up feel lacking and needy, imagine the power of marketing that's targeting our kids. Really; imagine it.

Now imagine how hard you'll need to fight to stop their outlook on life being tainted by big business. They're being bombarded by millions of messages a year about the importance of different products in their lives—how many messages are they getting from you?

Tell your kids how it is. Fill in the back-story for them; trace the links between marketing, merchandising and manipulation. Teach them about restraint and moderation and 'appreciating what you have' by practicing it yourself, and by encouraging every attempt they make to move down that same path. Keep up with the news, and read stories with them about products gone wrong, about body-damaging nanoparticles in cosmetics, about factory sweatshops and the true environmental and social cost of items on their wish list.

Wising up your children to the ways of marketing gurus will benefit both them and the planet. It will save them and you a whole load of money, it will build lots of self-respect, and it will save the environment from a whole lot of damage. Knowledge about marketing gives kids the empowerment to say, "No, I don't need that."

Knowledge about the ins and outs of marketing means the items they finally decide to buy will represent a whole lot more value and bring them and others a whole lot more joy and fulfillment.

THOUGHT LAUNCHERS & CONVERSATION STARTERS

- The next time your child is offered a free gift at a business find some time later to discuss with them whether it was just the people being kind, or if the business might have had another reason for doing/providing what they did. Ask them to think of **the real cost** of the free gift they've been given (e.g., a free toy at a fast-food chain uses up lots of precious resources and creates pollution in its manufacture and transport; a balloon from a bakery might end up in the ocean, etc.). It's definitely difficult to strike the balance between being an annoyingly authoritarian parent and a parent who can gently encourage their child to think for themselves—but it can be done. Perhaps one day your child will surprise you and tell the storekeeper, "No thanks, I don't need that, but thanks anyway."

- Get a notepad for your children (or better still, make one yourself by clipping together cut-up, recycled paper!) and have them do an **'undercover spy project'** in which they write down the name of every company whose marketing message they've seen during the day. Both you and they will be amazed...from food packaging to car logos, billboards to product placement in movies, T-shirts to taxi cabs, radio jingles to running shoes, advertising is everywhere.

- Next time one of your children tells you they want something because it's super cool, remind them that it's only super cool because **a bunch of grown-ups in suits** have decided that it is. Maybe talk about some of the things they used to think were cool, and 'had to have', and where they are now—stuffed in a drawer, chucked in the bin.

- Pick out an everyday item in your house, like a cereal bowl, and ask your kids how they would go about selling 10 million of them to other kids. What messages and mediums would they use, what celebrities, what competitions, what fears and weaknesses would they exploit? This puts them in the **marketers' shoes** and helps them realise what they're falling victim to themselves.

- Discuss with your children how marketing adds to the **cost of the products** they buy. Talk about the millions of dollars that are spent on marketing rather than making the products cheaper or better or longer-lasting, or the fact that more money is spent on marketing in most companies than on research and development.

- When buying gifts for other children, encourage your own children to think about giving an unbranded gift or a hand-made or **homemade** one.

- Discuss the concept of **appearance vs. achievement**.

- Ask your children to think of ways in which they can increase their happiness that **don't rely on 'things'**, e.g., developing friendships, learning new skills, caring for a pet, etc.

- Have your children cut out or watch some ads and ask them to think about the **legitimacy of the claims** made in the ads (is the product really environmentally friendly, or the best, or the cheapest? Will it really make you happier, slimmer, win you more friends, etc.).

- Help your children **research everyday things** we do to see if they were originally introduced by marketers, such as the now cultural norm of women shaving their armpits (perhaps encouraged by razor companies?).

- Ask your children to decide if the **emotions ads evoke** are really relevant to the product, e.g., if a soft drink's ad is based on the theme of healthy-looking people of different ages and from different countries coming together and having lots fun in a pristine natural environment with great upbeat music in the background, how is this relevant to a product that potentially could have an immense negative global impact (e.g., health issues, use of non-renewables in the manufacture and distribution of its product, product pollution, etc.).

- Invite your children to create 'anti-ads' wherein they list all the things an advertiser has left off an ad on purpose (e.g., no one really needs this product to go about their day-to-day life; the parent company has just made 250 people redundant; they're using non-renewable resources to make and ship the product; the product and plastic packaging will end up in landfill; the actual manufacturing cost is 1/10th of the price of the product, with the rest going to multinational shareholders; the company doesn't pay its fair share of taxes in your country; if you use too much of the product it will have negative consequences for your health, etc.).

The aim of the above exercise is to encourage your children to think critically, so that they'll be able to make up their own minds about ads throughout the course of their lives. Ads are meant to target our emotions, so it doesn't mean they can't sing along and enjoy them—some ads are just great—but we do need our kids to be able to distinguish between creativity and truth, between niceties and necessity.

The added advantage of teaching your children these methods of deduction is that they'll be able to put them to good use when self-regulating their purchasing decisions. They'll be able to run through all the pros and cons of a product or service before committing to it.

In conclusion, we all have free will. We can say "no" to buying products. We can choose not to succumb to marketing—and our children must, if they're to save their money, reduce their consumption of the world's resources, limit their own personal contribution to pollution and draw their own conclusions. They need to know that it's okay to 'swim against the tide', but it's not easy, thanks to the ruthlessness and invasiveness of most marketing in our society. Our kids will need all the help, encouragement and advice they can get to extract themselves from the current system that has dumbed down the whole notion of 'free choice' to 'the right to buy whatever we tell you that you want'.

Chapter 17

USING TIME WISELY

For disappearing acts, it's hard to beat what happens to the eight hours supposedly left after eight of sleep and eight of work.

DOUG LARSON

You may delay, but time will not.

BENJAMIN FRANKLIN

Be Prepared...the meaning of the motto is that a scout must prepare himself by previous thinking out and practicing how to act on any accident or emergency so that he is never taken by surprise.

ROBERT BADEN-POWELL

"I'm bored," say the kids.
"I'm excited," say the parents.
It's only when kids get bored that they have time to think creatively. These days, kids are suffering from extracurricular overload. We drive them from tutoring to sport to birthday parties to music

lessons to gym to play dates, finally plopping them exhausted on the couch in front of a screen.

We give them pre-made doll's houses, lifelike ovens and custom-built cubby houses when we could just be giving them cardboard boxes and crayons.

Part of becoming a self-reliant adult means being able to produce one's own entertainment, rather than just consuming the entertainment manufactured by others.

By letting our kids get bored, and then giving them materials instead of the final product, we encourage their interest, their creativity and their thinking skills. Sure, we have to put up with 30 minutes of the increasingly hysterical "I'm bored" mantra, but if we can wait it out, before you know it, our kids find a way to entertain themselves. They might get busy in their bedroom, or lie on their back watching the clouds, they might start writing or painting or organising or planning a show, but if we never give them the space or the time, they never discover their inner boredom-buster.

Parenting can be a little boring at times too! 'The days can be long but the years are short' is a saying that hits the parental experience of time right on the head. How true this saying is, especially when children are small and we parents are sleep-deprived. A few hours can seem interminably long. Then, in a blur, our toddlers are teenagers, and then our teenagers are middle-aged! Given that we know the tricks time plays, we need to seize upon and enjoy the moments with our children now, because suddenly, they won't be just a year older, but a decade or more.

So, how long have we got? How long do we have left to walk this planet, to breathe its air, to love our beloveds, to enjoy the fresh air on our faces? How long have we got to be the best we can be, to make a difference, to raise children who will do good, not just well, to smile and be smiled at? How long until it is our turn to be eulogised, memorialised, farewelled?

I haven't a clue, but thinking about it sure helps one focus on living life now, on living life well, on living life with passion!

Would we spend weeks whingeing about an insult if we knew we only had weeks to live? Would we spend days fretting about fashion and furniture if we knew we only had days left? Would we spend minutes making mean or jealous comments under our breath if we knew we only had minutes to live?

Time is so precious, but it seems we only remind ourselves of that when someone we know dies. Then, days after the funeral, we go straight back to our old existence, even though we know we should and could be living in a more fulfilling, more purposeful way.

Challenge yourself to make the most of your time here. That doesn't mean being busy every minute of the day, in fact, it might actually mean cutting down on what you are doing! It's about living your life, not filling it.

Help your children understand that every minute is precious, and that wherever possible it shouldn't be wasted on gossip or bitterness or bad feelings. Sure, these feelings will be felt and expressed occasionally, but it's the hanging on to them and emphasising of them that poisons.

Choose today to introduce the concept of limited time to your children so it will help build their perspective about life.

For example, next time one of your children is fixated on something negative, perhaps ask them, "Do you really want to spend your time on this planet worrying about X when you could be doing Z?" Or, "Okay, so we've spent 20 minutes feeling sorry for ourselves. That's 20 minutes we'll never have again, so why don't we use the next few minutes to try something different?"

Some Buddhist teachings say that the only way to be happy is to live right in the present moment; not thinking about the past, not thinking about the future, but being present, right here, right in this moment.

I love this idea, and when I find myself 'spending time' with the kids, rather than 'being present' for the kids, this jolts me back to where I need to be; wholly in the moment. I'm switched on and tuned in, and the kids know they're really being heard, really being played with, really being parented.

It's not easy though, because I find it very hard to relax if I haven't planned ahead, whether it's planning dinner, figuring out when I'm going to get a chance to put out the laundry between rain showers, or how we're going to pay the bills this month! Obviously I'm not enlightened, because I also struggle with the idea that thinking about the future is not appropriate; after all, a lot of this book is about future thinking!

The concept of time is also interesting when you think about how it affects the way our countries are governed. It's hard for our leaders to make wise decisions when the timeframe on which they base those decisions is just the next brief electoral cycle.

At home, it's hard to get our children to concentrate for more than a few minutes when they're conditioned to watching short music videos and snippets of shows. And for us adults, it's difficult to extend our own thinking to plan a way out of debt when we have monthly bills to pay, seemingly constant unexpected expenses, and our kids moving up a size in shoes every other week.

Giving our children an appreciation of time, and in particular its incredibly limited nature, will hopefully help tune them in to making the most of each day, each relationship and each new experience. Giving our children an appreciation of time will connect them with history, the present, and the future. Giving our children an appreciation of time will mean they'll be able to perfect their own blend of imagining a moment, preparing for the moment and living life in the moment.

Being aware ourselves of how quickly time flies might also prompt us to prepare for the not-so-far-away future, and the various challenges that we and our children may come to face. For example, it takes a long time to earn the trust and love of a community—our own honeycomb—and we never know when we might need to call on it or to give it, so we should commit to starting to build those relationships right now.

Emergencies are called that because they happen suddenly or urgently, or are unforeseen. Part of my reason for writing this book is to hopefully nullify the unforeseen part! Time is on your side right now to prepare your family for events that may come to pass.

The first part of this book has hopefully helped you to *anticipate* some of the challenges your children may face. By researching further and learning more about your local area, you'll be better able to *assess* your options. *Prevention* might not always be up to you, but *preparation*—well, that's definitely up your alley.

People try to put money away for a rainy day. We insure our houses and contents 'just in case' something happens. We school our kids to help prepare them for adult life. We get ready for a big night out by choosing clothes and shoes that we'll enjoy wearing. We plan our next holiday, our renovations, and our garden beds, but for some reason, planning for emergencies isn't high on our list of priorities, but it's time it was.

While I was writing this chapter, a few towns just two hours north of us were cut off by floodwaters for a couple of days. At first glance, it seemed manageable—a couple of days; no worries—but after the floodwaters receded, life didn't return to normal as quickly as expected. The water treatment plants in the area had been compromised by sewage, so people were advised not to drink the water until further notice. As days turned into weeks, this caused a lot of hardship and angst for people who had no stored/potable water available. Of course, it wouldn't have bothered someone who had spent some time planning in advance and who had seen the wisdom of having either water barrels tucked away or a small, portable water filter in a drawer.

When disaster strikes, we tend to think that someone in authority will take care of us and put everything to rights, but what if a disaster meant that the other 10,000 people in the neighbourhood were also lining up for that care? What if help was slow in coming, and recovery took months? Wouldn't it be great if you didn't need to add your family to the scramble for assistance; if your family, rather than being the victims, were able to help the victims; if you were part of the solution rather than part of the problem?

There's a motto on one of the survivalist-type websites: "Better to be prepared early than a minute too late!" It sums up the value of thinking ahead. But who has the time to put together a family emergency plan? We all do, of course; we just have to make it a priority. It's so worth it.

You can live your life practically free of worry if you plan and lay a foundation that makes you feel comfortable and secure and hopeful. You can also save a lot of money by calmly preparing in advance for an emergency, rather than being one of the panicked masses after the event.

How does all this relate to helping your children understand the value of time? Hopefully, by making some small preparations, you and your children will feel confident that you will have time, will have a future! You'll have a feeling of peace and contentment that if something were to go wrong, you'd be able to handle it, because you've taken action and are prepared.

The best emergency preparedness you could ever do though is to forge strong ties with your own family, neighbours and community. The time to make a start on that, future-proofing your family and being the best you can be, is right now.

Oliver Wendell Homes once said, "Many people die with their music still in them. Why is this so? Too often it is because they are always getting ready to live. Before they know it, time runs out."

THOUGHT LAUNCHERS & CONVERSATION STARTERS

- Instead of filling the children's week with endless after-school activities, make sure they have plenty of **time to do nothing**.

Let them get bored, whinge about it for a while, and then come up with their own way to 'unbore' themselves!

- Have everyone in the family do up a **seven-day time diary** so you can all see what you spend your time doing. If you're spending too much time in one area that isn't giving you a lot of fulfilment and/or isn't moving you toward your goals, work out how you can spend less time doing that thing!

- **Celebrate the start of each new season** with your children so as to get them in touch with nature's rhythms. Hold a little party at the beginning of each season and have them note the differences in nature, depending on whether it is spring, summer, autumn or winter. Midway through each season, have them write down their favourite and not so favourite elements of it.

- Take some time now to think about some of the decisions you make that will be of benefit or detriment to the as-yet **unborn people** of the world.

- Enjoy the freedom of a **schedule-free day**. Pick a day, keep it free for the whole family, take your watch off and enjoy life at your own pace.

- Have a **go-slow day**. Do what you normally do, but do it slower. Walk to the shops to buy food, make a meal in a slow cooker, play a board game with the kids instead of an electronic game, read books instead of watching TV. Notice how you enjoy what you do more when you truly make time for it.

- Try living life at a **different pace** for a while—faster as well as slower than you normally would—and experience the difference.

- Work out a way to '**make memories**' for your children. What special things can you do as a family that they'll be able to remember and enjoy for a long time to come?

- If your children are engaged in a multitude of after-school activities, ask them which one is their absolute favourite, and maybe drop some of the other activities so you can make time to **teach them 'invisible' skills** like cooperation, patience, empathy, problem-solving, etc. Sometimes we get so wrapped up in teaching our kids formal skills like tennis, piano, and ballet that we forget the importance of the life skills we parents can model.

- **Every day is a new day**; every day gives us the opportunity to make positive changes. Don't wait life out sitting on the sidelines!
- Ask the kids what the **top five useful items** are that your family would need if you had to live for five days without power, water or the ability to leave the house.
- Have the kids help you **pack an emergency kit** so they know what's in it, where to find it and how to use the items inside. Discuss with them why you're preparing the kit, explain to them that it's not because you're expecting something to happen, it's just so that if anything ever did, you'd be okay. Let them know that, just like we brush our teeth to prevent cavities, and look both ways before we cross the road to prevent being run over, **it's wise to prepare for an emergency**, just in case.
- Ask the kids how many toilet rolls they think your family would need for a month (kids always love **toilet humour!**).
- Set up a **family emergency plan**, so that everyone in the family knows what to do if disaster strikes. Where would we meet? How would we communicate? What would we do?
- **Set the kids some survival challenges**, e.g. they have 24 hours to produce half a cup of drinkable water that hasn't come from a tap. They could research how to do this on the Internet.
- With the understanding that our time on earth is limited, read Jack Canfield's *The Success Principles—How to Get From Where You Are to Where You Want to Be* and get moving on **clarifying and acting on your life purpose.**

Chapter 18

ROME WASN'T BUILT IN A DAY

Frankly, I'm more worried about the violence we do to ourselves and our children by allowing the media to create an expectation of instant gratification.

HUGH MACKAY

As we get past our superficial material wants and instant gratification we connect to a deeper part of ourselves, as well as to others, and the universe.

JUDITH WRIGHT

The belief that we can rely on shortcuts to happiness, joy, rapture, comfort, and ecstasy, rather than be entitled to these feelings by the exercise of personal strengths and virtues, leads to legions of people who in the middle of great wealth are starving spiritually.

MARTIN SELIGMAN, PhD

Beekeeping is a pursuit that requires patience. When you start with a nucleus colony of bees, you need to let them build up their strength and honey stores before winter hits, so it's rare that you'd take honey in that first season. Then the next year comes along and again you must wait until the conditions are right and there's a honey flow before you can enjoy nature's liquid gold. But from the perspective of a bee, the gratification should be delayed as long and enjoyed as exquisitely as possible, because it takes a bee its entire life to produce just 1/3 of a teaspoon of honey.

"I want it and I want it now!" said Veruca Salt in Roald Dahl's *Charlie and the Chocolate Factory*, and so say many children (and their parents) today.

Instant gratification is more about self-interest, self-indulgence, and fleeting excitement than about collaboration, persistence, patience and long-term satisfaction, but it's these latter ideals that our children need to embody if they're to live a fair and fulfilling life.

"Take it today with nothing to pay!"

"36 months interest free."

"Delivery today."

"Grab and go."

Marketing messages shout at our children that they should have it all and have it now. University grads enter the workforce and are disheartened when they haven't worked their way to the top by the end of the first year. Friends lament when two weeks of dieting doesn't melt away two years of excess. And we've all felt the temporary high of an impulse purchase, only to experience the long-term low as we struggle to pay it off, while it becomes clutter, or ends up being turfed for something newer.

A big influence on our children today is the instant gratification they obtain at the controls of electronic games. Playing computer games gives them a perceived level of control over cyber people, animals and purchases that they would never have in the real world. They come away from these games thinking they're great drivers, dancers and demon-slayers, and have little understanding of the paradox of time being so compressed and perceived achievements so inflated.

When so much of their time, energy and thought is invested in this cyber world, there's not much opportunity for patience, self-control or generosity, or perhaps it's just that this time spent online could be better spent learning how to communicate with and relate to real people, rather than their Facebook picture.

You want to buy a tractor for the farm game? Sure, a few minutes of pressing buttons and pretending to collect eggs will earn you what you need. Want to get somewhere in a hurry? Just knock that guy in the blue car out of the way. Want to be sociable? Sure, just spend three hours texting rather than actually go out and play or have lunch with friends. Want a new image? Easy, go on a shopping splurge, spend a limitless amount of money on new clothes, and while you're at it, change that natural hair colour of yours for something cooler, countless times!

Even the kindest, savviest of kids can't help being intoxicated by the sense of everything being in their control. They can't help but become desensitised to real-world violence. They can't help their desire to chase the next thrill. It's so easy to become addicted to the instant pay-offs delivered by spending time online, hooked up, wired in.

Happens in our family too! The other night we discovered that one of our resourceful daughters had taken a torch and a blanket and headed out to the office to play an online horse game at three am! She's desperate to get her own horse in the real world, and has been doing chores and saving up, yet the addiction of this online game is that she can buy and sell virtual horses at will. That's obviously way too tempting for a child still developing self-control.

If we allow our children to be game players, we need to regularly remind and show them that the real world is not like the computer world they play in.

In the real world, we need to wait, be patient, work hard, be persistent, and add value. In the real world, there's depth. There are feelings other than those associated with winning and losing, there isn't always a constant barrage of activity and excitement on offer, and if we want to be good at something, it takes years of practice, not one button-pressing hour. If we want people to do as we say, we need to be polite, understand their point of view and patiently persuade. We need to ensure that it's a win-win, not a win-lose. We can't just bump them off the screen, drive over them or zap them with our lasers. In the real world, it's give and take, not take, take some more, give it to 'em, boom!

When we groom kids from an early age to expect bonus points and instant pay-offs, it's easier for them to become despondent when they don't become overnight experts in baseball, board games and biology. When our children tell us they want a new gadget, and we get it for them instantly, they never learn about the benefits of goal-setting, savings plans, anticipation and patience. When they see us indulging in instant gratification ourselves, it makes it even harder for them to understand why it's not the best option in the long term.

Children of the screen need help adapting to the reality of the real world. The real world is slower. In the real world, communication and cooperation are more important than the speed of your thumb and index finger. And they need guidance so they can experience a healthier state of contentment than could ever be delivered by a computer chip.

Jump at opportunities to involve your kids in activities that teach cooperation, perseverance, and teamwork—all attributes needed for a successful, functioning hive. A good place to start is within your own family, because if they learn to carry their weight here, one day it will help them to carry their weight in society and contribute to the bigger picture.

Give your children plenty of opportunities to earn money, respect and thanks. By having the kids help you with the vacuuming, they're learning that they don't live in a vacuum! Don't feel guilty asking them to stop playing a computer game so they can help around the house. It's not going to rob them of their childhood; it's going to prepare them for their adulthood.

THOUGHT LAUNCHERS & CONVERSATION STARTERS

- Avoiding instant gratification doesn't mean avoiding **spontaneity**; have lots of unexpected fun with your kids!
- Have an **electronic-game-free month** at least a couple of times a year. Leave your children to their own devices without their devices! Plan some fun family activities. After they go cold turkey and the whining stops, notice the changes in your children and the mood of the house—you might just make it an electronic-game-free year after that!
- Ask your children to **commit** to doing one activity every day for five days (it might be making their bed, feeding the dog or some other activity of their choice). Reward their diligent commitment with an activity they enjoy doing with you.
- Ask your children to guess how many people and how long it took to build your house, a local landmark, and the pyramids in Egypt. Get them thinking about **effort**, commitment and time scales.
- Ask your children to think about professional athletes. See if they have any idea how many hours of how many days of how many years it took them to get where they are today. (Malcolm Gladwell, the author of *Outliers*, says it takes **10,000 hours of practice** to master something). Ask them what they might have missed out on along the way in order to achieve their current success, and what they've gained.
- Discuss a major purchase your family is considering making, and how you will **save for it**, rather than putting it on a credit card.
- Next time your children ask you to buy something for them, give them the opportunity to save for it themselves. They need to learn now that it is up to them to **work toward their dream**, that they shouldn't expect things to be handed to

them on a platter, and that they'll be so much more proud when they achieve it themselves.

- Ask your children to think about the thing that would give them the most pleasure right now. Then see if you can **expand that idea** to see what it might mean more broadly speaking, e.g., if they say they'd like a mobile phone, the bigger picture might be that they're seeking independence and self-reliance. What are some other ways of providing that?

Chapter 19
....
UNCONDITIONAL LOVE

*If we make our goal to live a life of compassion and
unconditional love, then indeed the world will become a
garden where all kinds of flowers can bloom and grow.*

Dr Elisabeth Kubler-Ross

*Love is the will to extend one's self for the purpose of
nurturing one's own or another's spiritual growth.*

M. Scott Peck

A nurse bee will check baby bee larvae around 1,500
times a day, nourishing them with whatever they
need to grow into healthy adults: pollen, honey, royal jelly. Now
that's attentive parenting! But bees aren't perfect. I've watched
fluffy baby bees trying to hatch while the adults literally walk all
over their faces!

What's your parenting style? Do you openly and tenderly show
love to your child? Are you gentle or irritable? Calm or spring-

loaded? Warm or cold? Nurturing or demanding? Consistent or inconsistent?

The love we show for our children, in how we hold them, how we speak to them and how we model behaviour for them, will have more impact on their lives than any other thing. Childhood is where adults are made.

It's the way children are raised that determines the future of their society. This is a wonderful thing, as it means that we parents hold the key to creating a wonderful future for our children. Likewise, it's the way other children are being raised and treated around the world that will also impact our own.

In Robin Grille's exceptional book *Parenting for a Peaceful World,* he writes:

"Genes might be thought of as the seed of a tree, while childhood represents the complex conditions that support and direct the seed's growth: the soil profile, the nutrients, micro-organisms and toxins in the soil, the climate and the precipitation. These environmental conditions sculpt the shape, size, colour, health and vigour of the tree, so that if cloned seeds were germinated under different conditions—one on the side of a dry cliff, the other in an alluvial plain, one in dry, mild weather, the other exposed to violent storms—these trees would look very different to each other."

In other words, how we raise our children is a far greater factor in their development than the genes they're born with. It's brought home to me every time I go beekeeping, because if I'm calm and feeling sunny, the bees normally respond in kind. If I'm stressed and impatient, that's what I get back.

Unconditional love doesn't mean letting our children get away with murder. Unconditional love is about loving them no matter if their skills and interests are different to ours. Unconditional love is about showing them a better way when they do wrong, and helping them strive to be the best they can be. It's about living for your children—by being who **you** are and also the best and most consistent supporters of who **they** are—not living through them.

Unconditional love is not about letting our children run riot. It's about providing guidelines and helping them take responsibility for their own actions. They can't do that if we keep telling them that it's someone else's fault. I can't count the number of times I've seen a child fall over or run into something and the parent goes up to the offending bit of footpath or furniture and says something like, "Naughty table!" This doesn't teach our kids to take care of themselves; it teaches them to blame external forces for any bad thing that befalls them. Maybe a more appropriate thing to say would be: "Whoops! Do you need some help getting up?"

Unconditional love is also about us. It's about being comfortable in our own skin, being kind to ourselves, and giving ourselves the power to grow. It's about feeling good about ourselves so we can feel good about—and do good for—the world.

We all have the power to choose love over hate, joy over despair, tolerance over judgement.

As parents, the love we share with our children every day does the same job as the elbow pads skateboarders wear—it gives them padding when things go wrong, and the confidence to try amazing things!

THOUGHT LAUNCHERS & CONVERSATION STARTERS

- **Reconnect.** Take a month off to travel as a family to find out who you all are free of the influences of TV, computers, work, school and peers. Don't head to a fancy resort and throw the kids in childminding; travel frugally within a three-day radius of your home. Try rock climbing, gold fossicking, hiking through National Parks. Visit all the libraries you come across. Along the way apprentice your family to an indigenous person, woodworker, farmer or artist. Volunteer at old peoples' homes and animal shelters and see where the road takes you. Discover the area in which you live, while you discover more about yourself and each other. Before you say "We can't afford to do that" or "There's no way I could get the time off work", work out a life so you can. Your children are only young now, so now matters.

- Think about why you're loveable. Write down at least 20 reasons.
- Ask your children to write down why they're loveable.
- Ask the kids to tell you why they think you love them, and then tell them another 10, 20, or 30 reasons why you do!
- Ask your children to write down the names of 10 people they love.
- Ask your children to write down the names of people, places and animals they feel a sense of love for, though they've never met them, been there or encountered them. Then work out a way to share some of your family's love with them.
- Any time, any place, call for a family hug!

Chapter 20

HOME TRUTHS

Rather than love, than money, than fame, give me truth.
HENRY DAVID THOREAU

If you tell the truth, you don't have to remember anything.
MARK TWAIN

'Veracity' is defined in the Macquarie Dictionary as 'truthfulness in speaking or statement; habitually observant of truth,' so that's the standard I intend to live by in this chapter, even though I know that not everyone will agree with what I have to say!

I don't know of any subject that gets parents more riled than that of how they talk to their children about Santa, death, the Easter Bunny, sex, etc., but my feeling is that if adults deserve the truth, so do children. We just need to do it in an age-appropriate way, and only to the level of interest that our children show.

Take the day my five-year-old son and I took delivery of our first bull on the farm. The cows all came over to see who the latest arrival was, and as soon as Mickey the bull was through the gate he did his thing. My son knew the basics of how to make babies, but he looked at me wide-eyed.

"Did you jump up on Daddy that way, Mum?" he asked seriously.

Of all the possible questions, I sure wasn't expecting that one, but it was a valid question, so I just explained that humans have sex in a variety of different positions, but not quite like Mickey the Bull. He didn't ask any more questions, so I figured that sex education was over for the day.

Death is another very personal topic to talk about. As a kid, I went to many funerals, whereas my husband didn't attend one until he was in his thirties. As a child, he didn't even attend his own father's funeral. Whether that was because they were trying to protect him, or he was trying to protect himself, I still don't know, but in comparison, my parents brought me up not to be scared of death, but to respect it. They wanted me to know that it was an inevitable part of life, something that couldn't be avoided. So, when the kids ask me, "Are you going to die before me, Mummy?" I can only tell them the truth, that everyone dies some time, but that I intend on sticking around as long as possible!

Our kids attended their first funeral a few months ago when my aunty died after a battle with cancer. Before we went in, I took them aside and explained that, although I would be bawling my eyes out in the church, I was okay, and they didn't need to worry. I explained that I would be crying because I loved Aunty Mary so much, that I would miss her, and that I wanted to celebrate her wonderful life because she was the coolest chick around!

It was a lovely ceremony, and you could tell she'd had a hand in planning it; she'd even left a special song to be played for my uncle. One of the most moving moments was when all the grandchildren went to the casket, on top of which was a rainbow of ribbons on spools. Each of them took one of the ribbons, which then unfurled as they fanned out through the pews and up the aisles and then tethered the ribbons at various points in the church. Some of the ribbons brushed over us as they were lifted higher, and it was as though Mary was amongst us. The children spoke about how the ribbons symbolised Mary's amazing spirit, her colourful personality, her depth. We sat under the ribbons listening to her favourite music for a while, and then my uncle was handed a pair of scissors and asked to cut them so as to release Mary from the earth and send her spirit soaring. It was a very, very moving moment, a heartbreaking moment, an acknowledgement of death, and an acknowledgement of great love, an acknowledgement that we had been left behind, and a realisation that for those who loved her, life, however different, would have to go on. That moment still gives me goose bumps, and I'm confident it was a positive experience for the children.

I know many people think it's a terrible thing to take children to a funeral, to expose them to death and suffering in such a way. On the contrary, I felt we were exposing them to life and love, and to loss, in a very gentle, solid way. We need to know about death in order to really embrace life and all its beauty, tragedy and joy.

Children also need to know that after tragedy and suffering and death, there is a future. They need to know that life goes on for those left behind. What I wish for my children is that when the time comes and it's my turn, after expressing their grief, they'll be able to carry on, heal, and make the world a better place by sticking with it. I don't want them to be angry at me for never preparing them for the truth of death.

Last weekend I took them to the cemetery to visit the memorial to the babies we lost to miscarriage. We all cried for the loss of siblings they would never know, but the conversation went in so many directions, from sadness to gratefulness, that overall, it was a very important and rewarding experience.

Two of my adopted brothers are buried in the same cemetery. Robert died when he was seven, hit by a car while on the pedestrian crossing outside our home. When my son realised he was the same age as Robert, he spontaneously reached over and hugged the headstone. My other brother, buried in the same grave, was in his forties when he died from a heroin overdose. Different beginnings, different opportunities, different endings, and a stark reminder that you only get one life, so make it the best you can, and be the best you can be.

Being gently truthful with our children also means that they'll trust our communications with them. Inviting their questions and spending time truly listening to their concerns strengthens our bonds more than any flash holiday or gift of new clothes could ever do.

We always answer their questions. They know they can ask us the meaning of swear words, but they also know that we've made a choice as a family not to use those same words. And when it comes to the question "Is Santa real?" we've taken the same honest approach, while trying to keep the magic and fun too.

We chose to keep the magic of Christmas alive by telling the children the original story of St Nicholas, his generosity to the poor, his spreading of joy. That's what we focus on. We talk about how we keep this spirit of goodness and celebration alive by preparing gifts for each other and coming together each year and by doing good deeds for strangers and people less fortunate than ourselves. We tell them that some people believe that to this very day he rides his sleigh across the world delivering gifts to the children of the world, that it is said there are reindeers with cool names and elves aplenty.

When the kids asked if the supermarket Santa was real, we asked them what they thought. "Nah, his beard doesn't look real." "Nah, 'cause if it was him, he should be at the North Pole getting ready." "Maybe..." So, it's been possible to keep the magic of Christmas alive without succumbing to being dishonest about who bought the presents.

I suppose the best gift we can give our children is to awaken in them a love for the magic that surrounds us. By being able to enjoy the magic of the everyday, their lives will be a lot more content than if they were being encouraged to believe in the magic of 'fantasy'. And there is magic all around. How else can you explain the colours of a rainbow, the beauty of a butterfly, the sound of a waterfall, the taste of fresh honey, the sky at sunset, and the cool breath of dawn? A child who can take pleasure in the little things doesn't need made-up, grown-up lies and commercialism to live a happy life.

Santa is an intensely personal issue, but so are the issues of drugs and sex and disease and violence, and all these can be dealt with truthfully but, at the same time, at a level suited to their age and not beyond their current level of interest.

I often wonder if protecting children from unpleasant truths helps them or hinders them. I wonder how much information we should expose them to, and if we should divulge good and bad news equally, or play up the good while downplaying the bad. In the end, it all seems to even out as it is meant to, because when you're tuned in to what you hope for the kids, you seem to know what to tell them, how much to tell them, and when to tell them. You seem to be in a place where the conversation is natural, flowing, wanted, needed and appreciated.

This book came about partly because, although I've done plenty of research in the past for business plans, balm recipes, medicinal plants and honey bees, I realised I was raising three human beings without putting in the same kind of research effort! Some of the things I discovered about oil, war, business, chemicals and more as I chased the truth threw me, and at times, the information I found made me feel anxious, nervous, cheated and angry. But having that foundation of knowledge has since led to joyous discoveries and a tremendous sense of wellbeing.

I suppose I'm one of those people who've always wanted to know. I haven't always accepted what's been written in the paper, what my teachers told me to believe, what my boss asked me to do. I think I've been driven to question things so I can find a solid base upon which to construct my life. Of course, this has made me quite a pain for my parents, teachers and bosses at times, but it has set me up to appreciate why our children need to know the reasons for decisions, the history behind actions, and the prejudices and self-interest that can colour what is held up as gospel.

When I was growing up, my parents would often lay down the rules, but wouldn't go into much detail about why we had those rules. I wanted back story, and that's why I now like to talk with my own kids about the ins and outs of our decisions and actions. One of the stumbling blocks to this is knowing how much information to give a child, and when to start with all the details. I figure the best time to start is now, rather than waiting, because it's not as though kids suddenly switch on at a certain age.

By starting young and sharing your values and the reasoning behind them with your children, you give them a framework with which to build their own sets of beliefs and rules to live by. By not always talking in black and white, and by acknowledging that there's often more than one way to approach a problem, you help them to remain flexible in how they approach different problems and personalities. They start to get a feel for the playing field, the options, the consequences and the rewards.

'Telling the truth' is a quality we value so much in our children that it is up to us to model truthful behaviour for them. If we want honesty and trust, that's how we need to live. If our kids hear us saying something mean about a neighbour, and then see us chatting to them like we're best friends, they know that we're not being truthful.

If we're unable to apologise to our children when we've done something wrong, we're not being honest with either them or ourselves, and they sense that.

Teaching our children to be truthful with themselves, and helping them to find their own truths, is an important part of being a parent. As grown-ups, we understand that there are reasons why kids fly off the handle or treat a sibling meanly, but they aren't yet old enough to be so self-aware. Discussing with them what might be behind their actions helps them connect deep within themselves, rather than with their facade.

I feel that children who can trust their parents' truthfulness—and enjoy all the benefits that such an honest relationship brings—will have a much better chance in the future than those for whom truthfulness is just something that gets in the way of a good story.

THOUGHT LAUNCHERS & CONVERSATION STARTERS

- Invite your children to **ask** you five questions a week to which they want a completely truthful answer…and then be truthful!
- Think deeply and have a bit of fun about how your family is going to handle discussions about **life, death, Santa and the tooth fairy.**
- Next time you don't know the answer to something, grab a book, find an expert or get on the Internet to help find **the truth.**
- Encourage a bit of **skepticism**—not cynicism—in your children. The Skeptics Society applies reason "to any and all ideas—no sacred cows allowed. In other words, skepticism is a method, not a position. Ideally, skeptics do not go into an investigation closed to the possibility that a phenomenon might be real or that a claim might be true. When we say we are 'skeptical,' we mean that we must see compelling evidence before we believe." There's even a Junior Skeptic publication available at www.skeptic.com/junior_skeptic/.
- Whenever you get the chance, let your children know how much you appreciate and **value their honesty.**
- Retell the story of *The Boy Who Cried Wolf* with your children. It's a great way to get the message of **truth and consequences** across.
- When a suitably minor incident occurs, let your children know that there will be **no punishment** if they tell the truth

(and you need to stick to that!), but if you find the truth has not been told, the consequences will be amped up.

- Ask your children to tell you some of the reasons **why telling the truth is important.**

- Be honest about how honest you are with your children. Are you a good **role model for truthfulness,** and if not, how can you become one?

- Talk to your kids about 'tactful' truthfulness. **Role-play** some situations with them, e.g., "You go to your friend's house for dinner and they serve you a meal you really don't like. Their mum asks you what you thought of the meal. What do you say?"

- Whenever you can, at bedtime give each child the opportunity to ask you **three questions** they really want answered. Answer them truthfully. This has been a great opportunity in our house to find out what's really on our kids' minds, what's troubling them, what's intriguing them, what they're looking for guidance on!

- Get a book out from the library about **body language,** and teach your children how to discern when someone is not telling them the truth. This will really help them hone their 'people radar'.

- Explain to your kids the meaning behind Mark Twain's quote (at the beginning of this chapter). Let them know that being caught in a lie can have huge consequences down the track, but more importantly, let them know that if they appreciate honesty in others, and if they enjoy **the feeling of trust,** then that is what they too must give.

Chapter 21

IT'S ALL IN THE DELIVERY

*What the caterpillar calls the end of the
world the master calls a butterfly.*

RICHARD BACH

When I realised that the way I lived my life was neither sustainable nor really commendable, and that there was actually a more fulfilling way to live, it set me on a path of discovery as I listened, read and learned more about everything from oil wars to food production, climate change to consumerism. The more I absorbed, the more I wanted to share what I'd learned with friends and family.

Big mistake! Talk about crash and burn! My delivery was always way off or just totally unwelcome. I kept forgetting that people are at so many different stages in their own journey. I suppose introducing some concepts to people is a little like introducing a new queen to a beehive. If you just put her in there, she'll be attacked, but if you give the bees a chance to get used to the idea, they'll eventually be open to potentially accepting her. With bees, you do this by placing her in a queen cage, then putting the whole cage in

211

the hive. One end of the cage has a small plug made of a sweet bee candy that the bees begin to chew through. By the time the opening is wide enough for bees to enter and exit, the queen's pheromones have gone through the hive and her presence is accepted.

Sometimes though, concepts outside the norm take longer to circulate and be accepted. That's because we all live in our own little worlds within a very big one. It's like those little Russian dolls, each layer revealing something smaller within:

— universe — planet — nation — state — city — town
— street — house — room — human body — brain
— personal history — media consumed — circumstances
— mood — thought — counter-thought, etc.

Timing also has a lot to do with it. When I showed them an early draft of this book around two years ago, friends scoffed at the thought of a modern-day nuclear disaster, that oil prices would affect how much they drove or that everyday citizens might be affected by climate calamities and a cash crunch. But now as I add the finishing touches to the book, there's a bit more nodding of heads than shaking of heads.

Everyone's experience is so different, and everyone's thought process so unique, that you can't just tailor one message even within your own family. People's realities and motivations and circumstances are so personal that there is no one size that fits all. But when you really understand the reality of things like peak oil, synthetic chemicals and the ramifications for the planet of trying to support seven billion people, there's no use keeping the information to yourself, because we really are all in this together.

But when it comes to our kids, how can we help them get the message without scaring them or making them feel helpless in the face of the issues?

It feels like kids are actually born with an awareness of and yearning for the bigger picture by the questions they ask and the curiosity they show, and it's we adults and the world we've created for our children that actually narrow this curiosity and potential sense of overall perspective. It's definitely time for reverse gear!

Our kids get the message by seeing, hearing, sensing, experiencing, sharing, laughing and exploring, not through lecturing, forcing, insisting, demanding, griping, moping and yelling. Note to self: got to stop that! ☺

As no one actually knows what the future holds for each of us, we can't promise our kids that it will stay the same economically, environmentally or socially. It wouldn't be fair to raise them thinking that everything will be better or that everything will be worse. What we can promise them though, is that if they give it a good shot, their lives will be fulfilling and rewarding.

Sure, their world will come with its own unique challenges, but that's what makes life interesting! I often say to my children, "How could you appreciate and really celebrate the good days if there was never a bad day to compare them with?" It's about enjoying what you have and making the most of it.

Anxiety can wreck the lives of both children and grown-ups. Its nasty combination of worry and nervousness leads to feelings of helplessness and depression. It cuts off optimism and the ability to be generous, and it diminishes happiness and the positive role we can play in the lives of our family and community. By role modelling for our children and showing them that good can come from bad, they won't slip into an anxious spiral. As Napoleon Hill said, "Every negative event contains within it the seed of an equal or greater benefit."

If kids come to believe that they don't have any control over their future or the world in which they live, they'll likely turn into sombre, depressed adults who feel that any contribution they make is worthless. They'll be fearful, cynical, insecure, negative, and unlikely to take any action. That's no way to live. That's why we need our children to know that the human spirit is remarkable, that there's magic in the world, that there will always be beauty, and that hope is eternal.

So, how do we paint a non-threatening or, better yet, an uplifting picture of the world for our children? How do we help our children grow up to be able to accept and embrace change, the best and the worst? How do we encourage them to be proactive, and contributors? How do we fill them with hope rather than hate, with spark rather than dark?

First, we can't take ourselves or the issues at hand too seriously. Yes, what's happening around the world is serious, but even people with a terminal illness can find relief and peace in laughter. Poke fun at yourself, laugh when you fail, show your kids that life can be more comedy than tragedy. Choose mischief over misery, grins over grimaces, sweet over sour. And do this every day.

Someone has walked dirt in all over the carpet, but is it really the end of the world? You're tired after another foul day at work, but if the reason you're working is to give your children a certain lifestyle, aren't they worth smiling at? You and your partner are at the end of your tethers over another backchatting incident, but instead of blowing your top, try softening up and share with your child the story of a time when you backchatted your own parents, why you did it and how you felt.

You can't and shouldn't laugh at everything in life, but by choosing to look on the bright side, you're sending a powerful message to your children about the ability to cope, and giving them a strong example of how venting can be done in a positive way.

When you're ready to start passing on some of your stronger philosophies about life—and I'm not talking about your set way of stacking the dishwasher—it's important to look for openings in casual conversation, as children can be quite receptive to thoughts shared through banter.

Using similes can help kids by relating an abstract concept to something they know, e.g., "Life can be like a really bumpy road sometimes, but it's still worth going on the trip!"

Kids who can adapt will do well in the years ahead. Kids who can go with the flow, who realise that even though they planned on 'A' happening, they'll also be able to cope when 'B' turns up, will be much more successful than those who've never experienced adapting to change.

It's not always easy though. Some kids just seem to have personalities that can go with the flow, while others find change irritating and debilitating. You need to work at it though, because change is going to be the only thing that stays the same in the coming years!

We thought our parents and grandparents had to deal with a vast amount of technological change, but they dealt with change that was mostly seen as being for the better at the time, electric washing machines, cheap international flights and affordable cappuccino machines, even computers and the Internet, to name a few! The change our children are going to have to deal with will be just as fast and furious, but perhaps will be more of a winding back than a winding up.

By helping our children understand that even though they may not have control over all the situations they will face, but that they do have control over how they react, we give them power to cope.

When children know that they're in control of their reaction to situations, though not the situation itself, they're empowered to move towards a healthier place. When they know they can choose to swap negative reactions for positive ones, they no longer feel powerless. Sure, they might want to keep whingeing for a while, but they also know that it's their choice to do so.

A great lesson for ourselves as well as our kids is that thoughts—unlike facts—are flexible, and that we have the power to focus on them, toss them, swap them, minimise them, morph them or turf them for better ones.

It's harmful to belittle our children's fears, or to make them feel stupid or ignored, but it's wonderful to show them how to dissect their thoughts so they realise there's a difference between *feelings* and *facts*.

215

A child who's afraid of sharks, and therefore won't go swimming, needs to have their fear acknowledged—of course no one wants to get eaten by a shark! But then you need to assuage that fear by presenting the facts to them, e.g., most shark attacks occur at dawn or dusk, so you can minimise your risk by not swimming at those times of day, and most sharks would prefer a feed of fish, not Felicity or Frank, etc.

I'm constantly learning as I hear other views and absorb research that alters my basic knowledge, interpretation and understanding of what I thought to be true. Everytime I truly listen to someone, and therefore truly hear them, I learn something. This is especially true when I listen to my own kids, so listen to your children's fears. Figure out their blind spots. Tune in to their personal strengths and weaknesses, and adjust your delivery accordingly. It can be fun sometimes to hold family meetings to discuss important ideas, problems and solutions. If it's not something you do regularly, the kids will just love it, and will really pay attention. Their ability to contribute will make them feel great.

How you share news, insights and information with your children will definitely influence the type of adults they become, so keep it open, keep it upbeat, and keep it up!

THOUGHT LAUNCHERS & CONVERSATION STARTERS

- **Each child is unique,** so work out what kind of delivery works best for each individual in your family.
- Spend a day being **conscious of how often you smile** at your kids rather than scowling.
- **Actively listen** to your children's conversations and help them adjust their language when it's negative, e.g., encour-

age them to use 'a long time' in place of 'never', help them narrow down 'everyone' to a couple of names, etc.

- Hold a **family meeting** once a month where you discuss a 'big issue'. Make it a game, giving the kids voting cards so they can help choose how the family will approach the issue. Ask the kids for their solutions to the problem and thank them for their input (don't discourage them by telling them their answers are wrong, but add your own thoughts to theirs).

- Do you ever have thoughts along the lines of, "This is all too much for me. Why do I bother?" Well, if you want to enjoy life to the fullest, you need to bother. Take every chance you can to help your children learn the **language of hope**. If one of your children says, "Every kid at school hates me," you need to challenge the word 'every'. If your child says, "They never let me play," you need to challenge the words 'they' and 'never'. If your child says, "You always..." you need to challenge the word 'always'. I can still remember my mum teaching me the difference between the words 'need' and 'want'. We all need to be aware of how much language—and what we tell ourselves—matters.

- **Children learn best by being involved.** Actions speak louder than words, so next time you want to share some information with your children, work out the best way to get the message across.

- Like a fishing line dropped into the ocean, have you ever noticed how a phrase dropped into conversation days earlier can suddenly capture your imagination? Or how something you might barely have paid attention to suddenly arises from your subconscious? Or how watching someone doing something a little bit differently breaks through like nothing else? You need to work out the best way to deliver the basic information to your own children, so they can think and act on it in a way that **makes sense** to them.

- One of the reasons I decided to put all these ideas down on paper was I realised that many parents wouldn't have the time or headspace to do the amount of research, reading and experimentation our family were doing in the area of raising kids for a changing world. I know my delivery of the information is far from perfect, but I've given it a go. What are some ways you can **help spread the word?**

Chapter 22

FACING THE MUSIC

In every community, there is work to be done.
In every nation, there are wounds to heal. In
every heart, there is the power to do it.

MARIANNE WILLIAMSON

Responsibility means not blaming anyone or anything
for your situation, including yourself. It is the ability to
have a creative response to the situation as it is now.

DEEPAK CHOPRA

Never doubt that a small group of thoughtful, committed people
can change the world: indeed, it's the only thing that ever has.

MARGARET MEAD

Xylophones, guitars, drums, birds, buzzing bees, the wind, waves...whatever the source of the sound, I want my children to be able to hear the music in this world, but they're only going to get a chance to do that if we stand up and face the music right now.

'Facing the music' means accepting the unpleasant consequences of our actions. It's only by accepting our shortcomings that we can be free to forgive them and do something about them.

Basically, once we decide to do something differently, we've faced the music, and everything—opportunities, perceptions and outcomes—starts to shift. And a shift is exactly what our children need from us.

The 'music' I faced was the way I perceived and lived in the world. I realised that the way I lived was based on the past, and on the here and now, with no thought for the future, or for anyone else, for that matter.

For some reason, volatile oil prices provided the wake-up call for me. This helped me to go back and dissect everything I thought I knew about life, business, government, climate change, society, the environment, cosmetics, food and family, and to retest those assumptions for their usefulness, truthfulness and relevance.

It also awakened me to the fact that I didn't have to be a passive member of the human audience. It prompted me to realise that our kids really do need guidance and leadership from me, their parent, rather than abdicating it to schools, commercial entities and peer groups. These days, even a perfectly healthy beehive needs constant and timely monitoring and assistance to help ensure it doesn't get overwhelmed by outside forces such as small hive beetles, parasitic varroa mites and disease. Our children are the same.

So, how about facing the music, and making a new set of resolutions from which you and your family can begin to compose your own special theme tune?

All it takes is for us to question our long-held beliefs about abundance, to look more critically at the lifetime of marketing messages we've soaked up, and to think about not just ourselves and our children, but their children and their children's children.

We don't need to be world leaders, rainforest activists or senior scientists to make a difference; we just need to enter into and see that bigger picture. We can start with ourselves by reducing the pollution we create, extending the life of resources and shifting our values from consumption to community. We can even save ourselves time and money by doing so! But we also need to go a step further, and start dragging governments and corporations along with us.

I went through a very dark grieving process when I realised the cascading effect that human greed will have on the world our children will inhabit. But I have also come out the other side.

In Clive Hamilton's book *Requiem for a Species,* he writes: "Despair, Accept, Act. These are the three stages we must pass through. Despair is a natural human response to the new reality we face and to resist it is to deny the truth, although the duration and intensity of despair means accepting the situation and resuming our equanimity, but if we go no further we risk becoming mired in passivity and fatalism. Only by acting, and acting ethically, can we redeem our humanity."

Once you face the music, you can jiggle to it.

THOUGHT LAUNCHERS & CONVERSATION STARTERS

- Sit down and **analyse your current lifestyle, happiness, and contribution** to the world. What would you like to change or enhance?
- Show your children how when you make a mistake, you can **learn from it** and choose a different path next time.
- **Make your own resolutions** and come up with 10 new resolutions for your family to try.
- Get your family together to decide what you can truly **commit to right now**, and what you can commit to implementing over the next week, the next month and the next year. Work out what preparation is required, who's going to be

responsible for it and how it can be made fun. Then, start implementing!

• Ghandi once said, **"Happiness is when what you think, what you say, and what you do are in harmony."** Think about how a quote like this might apply to you and your family.

• Here are just a few ideas to get you thinking about some areas in which your family can make a difference:

— **Using the car**
   Sit down with your children and work out how you can start using less oil now. For example, buy less items packaged in plastic, use more public transport, **minimise trips** to the shops, plan ahead so you can combine trips, cut out an after-school activity or ensure that you only sign up for after-school activities on the same day/in the same area/with other families who you can car pool with. Instead of owning a second car yourself, how about sharing one with other families in your street?

— **Prod your politicians**
   Make appointments with government representatives from local to state to federal. Prepare for the meeting with your family. Decide what you really want to say and what action you want taken. Then sit down with the politicians and let them know your concerns and **ideas for change.**

— **In the bathroom**
   Only wash your children's hair every third day to reduce both the in-your-face and hidden costs, i.e. the up-front cost of the product, the **reduction in energy and water use** associated with less showers,

and the reduction in chemicals on their scalps and being washed down the drain into the waterways! Once your current shampoo runs out, investigate switching to a natural shampoo and conditioner. We've had great fun experimenting with using basic shampoos and conditioner ranging from goat's milk soap to honey to apple cider vinegar!

— **Pay less attention to your looks**
Have you ever added up how much money you spend on make-up, haircuts and hair dye? Have you added up the hours you spend in the chair or in front of a mirror? How about the time it takes you to dry and style your hair? By paying less attention to your looks, you'll **save headspace, time and money** and you (and our waterways and soils and air) will be less likely to end up being negatively affected by synthetic chemicals.

— **In the kitchen**
Don't buy any prepackaged snacks for a month. Spend the money you save on **great ingredients** so you can bake your own.

— **At the takeaway**
Take your own non-disposable dishes or a **refillable** coffee mug rather than generating more plastic and polystyrene waste.

— **At the store**
Buy in bulk to save on packaging and to benefit from cheaper pricing. Write out a no-shopping list, a list of products you're going to **start boycotting** from now on. Take your own cloth or string bags.

— **At school**
Encourage your children's school to offer education that encompasses **ethics, philosophy and real-world skills.**

— **Give a little**
If you can't afford to donate money to a good cause, **donate your time,** or second-hand goods. If you don't have any of those either, get along to your local blood bank and donate some blood!

— **Speak up**
Take an interest in what's going on in your community, make contact with local organisations and speak up if you think there's a better, fairer way of doing things. Stage a protest or **support** someone else's!

— **For the animals**
Commit to reducing your family's meat and dairy **consumption,** which will in turn reduce suffering, energy depletion and pollution, and possibly even improve your health!

— **Make three days a week 'buy nothing' days**
That's right, commit to at least three **no-purchase days** a week.

— **Get useful**
Commit to learning a **new life skill** in the next six months, so that by the end of the year you'll be even more useful than you are now. Try something that you think you'll get a kick out of; sewing, home brewing, gardening, food preserving, beekeeping, first aid, or woodworking, for starters!

— **Make some music**

Go to a drumming workshop, buy a harmonica, organise a dance for families at your local hall, get in tune and **have some fun!**

— **Become a lightning rod for change**

When a single bee finds a great stash of nectar, she heads back to the hive to share the news. That encourages 10 other bees to take the journey to the flower. Then they go back and do a little waggle dance that encourages another 10. Soon the hive's all jigging away to the tune and filling up with goodness! You can become that pioneering bee; all it takes is for you to get enthusiastic and **spread the word** about ethical and environmentally friendly lifestyles, products, activities, services and people.

Chapter 23

YOU CAN DO THIS

If your actions inspire others to dream more, learn more, do more and become more, you are a leader.

JOHN QUINCY ADAMS

Only as high as I reach can I grow, only as far as I seek can I go, only as deep as I look can I see, only as much as I dream can I be.

KAREN RAVEN

Cultural change is a million acts of courage and kindness. That's the only way our culture has ever changed, and it's the only way it will change. And if you believe that, what that means is, you are a change agent, I am a change agent. We can be working every day, by the way we relate to the people we come into contact with, to make a very different culture, person by person, community by community.

MARY PIPHER, PH.D.

When someone takes a group photo, you might plant yourself front and centre, or like me, you might try and hide behind the tall guy so you're not in the shot! But in the big picture of life, we can't hide. We're in that image whether we like it or not. That being the case, we may as well make it a picture to be proud of.

You see, it's you. You're the key to opening the door right now to a great childhood and to successfully future-proofing your children. It's you who needs to be the futurist, imagining the skills, personality traits, community and choices that will help them successfully navigate the rest of their lives and steer a course for the good ship Earth.

It's you who needs to inject humour into everyday situations, to keep your head up when things aren't going well, to keep everything in perspective. If we adults don't persevere and show ingenuity, we can't expect our kids to.

We've all worked for a boss who wanted to keep us in our place; you know the type. He or she either gave us tasks so simple and dull they could have been achieved by the work-experience kid or, at the other end of the scale, set goals so completely unachievable we could do nothing but fail. But if you've been lucky along the way, you've also worked for a boss who empowered you, a leader who helped you expand your skills, put the necessary safety nets under your project, trusted you to use your judgement, encouraged you to give it your best shot and then asked you to analyse what worked and what didn't, so your next attempt would be even better. It was easy to see that he or she cared about you as a person, not just as a 'human resource'.

As parents, we're pretty much head of our own corporation, so, in your family, what kind of leader are you? When my dad read an early draft of this book, he said, "You really think a lot about being a parent, but you need to realise that kids will only learn by example."

"Dad, that would make it a one sentence book!" I replied.

The truth is, we don't wake up one day with all the answers. We're not perfect 24/7. We get tired. We get lazy. We get cross. We get distracted. We get greedy. We take the easy way out. We give in, give up, or give it to them! It takes a lifetime of learning, interacting, listening, trying and exploring to even get anywhere near the amount of knowledge, perspective, grace and wisdom we need to be able to guide our children, and by then, they're adults themselves! But my dad is right; it's what we do and how we do it, not what we say, that matters.

My children have seen me make incredibly poor decisions. They've seen me consume more of the earth's resources than is fair, they've seen me act uncharitably, gruffly and selfishly, but I'm working on myself every day so I can grow into a decent role model.

A few year's back my daughter asked me to show her teacher my skinned knees (I'd just played my first game of basketball after a 20-year hiatus, and it wasn't painless!). She looked at her teacher's reaction, and then announced proudly: "But she didn't give up. She didn't give up."

Sure, it had been a very amateur basketball game, and she'd seen me miss about 40 baskets, but she'd also seen the huge smile plastered all over my face as I enjoyed the challenge. She saw me apologise when I awkwardly bumped into people, she saw me keep going even though my face was redder than a summer tomato, and she saw me fall over and get right back up.

She got the message about perseverance, good sportsmanship and having a go because of something I had done and she had witnessed, and therefore absorbed. Soooo much is about us, our approach and our willingness to get involved, rather than staying on the sidelines.

We've been coached to be accepting, to let things slide, to support people's right to choose and make the wrong decisions—even if their choices kill them and others—while big business (and their shareholders) profit along the way. We've been taught by powerful marketing and economic forces that it's okay to be insipid, apathetic, wanting. We've been encouraged not to make a stand. We've been told that freedom of choice means we should have whatever we want, when we want it, and then be able to throw it away, without a thought for the rights of others. We've been told it's not cool to make a fuss about family, or to be strict, have values and feel spiritual. We've been told it's okay to make money from other people's misery.

Well now it's time for us to tell them something!

Be the Sherlock Holmes for your family, and get to the bottom of it; find the truth. Be the champion for your family, helping them to reach great heights. Be the safe haven for your family, equipping them with all they will ever need to be courageous, capable and kind. Be the voice for your family, and for all those to come.

In his book, *The Success Principles*, author Jack Canfield encourages people to "make a conscious effort to surround yourself with positive, nourishing, and uplifting people—people who believe in you, encourage you to go after your dreams, and applaud your victories. Surround yourself with possibility thinkers, idealists, and visionaries."

In addition to surrounding youself and your children with people who make you better people, also surround yourself with goals and affirmations and quotes that bring meaning and motivation. In the bathroom of my childhood home, my parents had a printed-out version of Max Ehrmann's poem *Desiderata*, which is Latin for 'desired things'. I read it practically every day, not really because I understood it, but because it was there on the wall above the toilet! Over time I absorbed it, and greatly admired its message. Think about the messages you'd like your children to start discovering and absorbing alongside you. Find a standard that you're excited to hold yourself up to. Firm up your philosophy of life, and live it every day. Be true to who you are and what you stand for.

If a single bee can make a difference and find a life-enhancing source of nectar for a whole hive, so should a single human be able to.

You *can* make a difference. You *will* make a difference. You *are* the difference.

THOUGHT LAUNCHERS & CONVERSATION STARTERS

- Set some time aside now to take up a **new hobby,** do a course or join a new group.
- Stop being so hard on yourself, and **celebrate your wins!**
- **Celebrate your failures too!** Give yourself a pat on the back for at least having the guts to give something a go. Learn any lessons from the experience and move on.
- **Forgive yourself** for what you have and haven't done, but give some thought to doing something differently today.
- **Try meditating.**
- Think about why you're here, and how you can contribute. If you don't have any idea, start making every effort to **find a positive purpose.**
- Visit websites such as www.ted.com and www.dolectures. com for **inspiration.**
- **Lead by example.** It's the little things that matter, like being thoughtful, like caring for the sick, like bringing joy into people's lives.
- Accept that **you have everything you need within you to start making a difference right now;** there's no need to wait.

Chapter 24

ZEST FOR LIFE

*True happiness comes from the joy of deeds well
done, the zest of creating things new.*

Antoine de Saint-Exupery

*When you dance, your purpose is not to get to a certain
place on the floor. It's to enjoy each step along the way.*

Wayne Dyer

Have you ever tasted a Thai curry with a wedge of lemon on the side? Or bitten into a lime zest cheesecake? Or savoured the precious honey of the Australian native stingless bee? Zingarama! It's a taste sensation, bursting with flavour, one that's surprising, awakening, tantalising, intense, satisfying. That's how our children can experience life and how we can experience it too!

When we rely on others, and on 'things', for our happiness, it's all too easy to turn on sullen airs, lapse into fatigue, or feel let-down, bored, angry or bitter. But if we choose to be players in life rather than spectators, we can make the most of every moment, even the difficult ones.

Bland might seem safe, and insipid might be non-threatening, but without some zing, some joy and delight, our children will plod along, never fulfilling their potential.

Have you ever been asked how your day has been, and replied with something along the lines of "Busy", "Long", "Okay", or "Glad it's over"? Conversely, you probably know people who, when you say, "What a lovely day," reply with "I suppose, but it's going to rain tomorrow!" It's as though we're ashamed to be having a good time! Well, stuff that in your pipe and smoke it! Life needs to be celebrated, not lamented!

I hope that our children will 'go for it', that they'll work out a way to stay true to themselves so they can be in their element as much as possible. I hope they'll be able to experience and exude competency, vibrancy, vitality, sparkle and wonder. Not every minute of every day of course, but certainly as many minutes as they can possibly squeeze in! I hope they'll be compassionate, caring, thoughtful, capable and able to keep things in perspective.

I think our kids have a good chance of achieving that if we help them develop their imagination and creativity, if we encourage them to feel grateful for all that they've been given, and all they can be, and if we show them that it's important to celebrate the small things, the good times, the moments.

Next time your dishwasher breaks down, the traffic is horrendous or the cat brings in a mouse, find something to celebrate, to laugh about. Turn the negative into a positive. Be joyful. Play 'it could have been worse' games.

Life is not just one big act, it's a series of scenes, of moments; good moments, mediocre moments, distressing moments, gentle moments. By teaching our children to find beauty in the current moment, you will find that they rarely wait until everything is 'perfect' before they allow themselves to enjoy life. They'll be able to enjoy the zest of life at will.

I've found that with beekeeping: the joy is not just at the end, when you taste the honey; it's in the process that starts with the ceremony of suiting up. There's comfort in the scent of the pine needles in the smoker, excitement at the sound of the bees humming, delight in the warmth of the sun during the walk to the hives, the anticipation of opening the lid...

There's a Zen proverb that says:

Before enlightenment
chopping wood
carrying water.

After enlightenment
chopping wood
carrying water.

I love this proverb, because it states so simply that it's all about our attitude. If we're sitting around waiting for some momentous change to shift our lives in a new direction, it ain't going to happen. We need to find the peace and the joy right now. We need to stop putting our lives off and make an effort to change the way we see problems right now. We need to seek and implement solutions that matter in the long term. We need to stop making excuses and start making choices.

We all know there are no guarantees. We and our children have had no choice as to the family we were born into and the country we grew up in, and we certainly don't know how we're going to die, or when. Uncertainty is what makes life interesting, edgy, and a never-to-be-repeated roller-coaster ride of thrills and spills, sadness and joy, achievement and adventure.

Encourage your children to embrace the unexpected, the difficult and the long term. Stand together as you reach out to the ill, the angry and the lost. Champion their efforts, whether it be a hunt for a snail or a Master's degree. Find a way to soften the edges of sharp predicaments. Foster usefulness and capability. Sing in the shower. Be silly. Be brave. Be upstanding. Give lots of hugs. Get lots of hugs. Get out there and get going! This is it, people! Throw that zest around and make a ruckus!

Afterword

In Malcolm Gladwell's book, *The Tipping Point*, he likens the spread of ideas and behaviours to that of a virus. That's exciting, because it means that great thoughts and moods and ways of doing things can spread like a contagion.

As the inequity and threats facing our world sink into people's awareness, I'm hopeful that positive change will come in a rush and head off or mitigate many of the threats discussed in the first part of the book.

I'm seeing it and feeling it around me now as more and more people in the suburbs, who have only ever turned their noses up at gardening, are now transforming themselves into green-fingered fanatics or trying their hand at chicken raising and beekeeping. Many are insulating their houses better, reaching out to their neighbours, and saying 'yes' to fresh food and free time rather than to processed, packaged food and a 24/7, TV-dependent, frenzied lifestyle. I'm seeing it in middle-aged people who are realising that life really is short, so they're going to spend the rest of theirs doing the things they love, rather than what they've been expected to do. And I've seen it in ninety-year-olds who are no longer buying pots of petrochemical moisturising goo, but are buying natural alternatives like balms from our farm instead. The exciting thing is, it's never too late, and it's certainly never too early.

I think it's really interesting that we've seen such an explosion in cooking shows, gardening shows and DIY shows, even shows devoted to good deeds, all the skills that we were starting to lose. It's as though people are subconsciously interested in returning to basic values, and the TV programmers and marketers have tapped into that groundswell. Then again, some of these shows might also have done more harm than good, creating unrealistic expectations for people who want the perfect house, meal and garden instantly. And anyway, food gets a little more complicated and a little less nutritious when you steam, roast, boil and flambé in "sauce d'evening" when you could just eat it raw!

"What must underlie successful epidemics, in the end, is a bedrock belief that change is possible, that people can radically transform their behaviour or beliefs in the face of the right kind of impetus," says Gladwell.

Well, we all know that change is possible, and there's certainly a lot of impetus going around!

We're ready for a tipping point that, instead of being exploited by marketers for business purposes, will be exploited by those seeking the betterment and enrichment of individuals, societies and the environment the world over. That's why you bought this book, because you're one of them. As your children's guardian, you have a huge stake in this.

I've felt an incredible sense of urgency to write this book, and not just because oil prices and electricity costs kept rising faster than I could type! It's because I'm passionate about equipping our family, and others, with the skills, ideas and attitudes that will help them to be part of the solution—or at least not part of the problem—to what sometimes seem like insurmountable issues and very real threats facing our people and our planet.

Whenever I slackened off on the typing, the 'breaking news' stories of intense storm systems, fires, financial disarray, unemployment, obesity, suicides, earthquakes, nuclear meltdowns, food shortages, rapidly declining bee populations and other beasties snapped me right back on track. Never before have I felt so passionate about a subject. Never before have I felt so lucky to be alive. Never before have I enjoyed the present and the promise of the future so much.

How cool is it that by empowering our kids, we make it possible for them to empower others, enjoy themselves more and make the most of their lives?! They'll still have their tantrums and tears (one of mine is throwing a massive and memorable wobbly right now and I don't think it's going to stop anytime soon!), but that's just part of growing up, testing the limits, being human.

So, thank you for reading this book. I really hope you and your family have discovered at least one cell of honeycomb that you'll be able to use to help launch your own unique journey of discovery, hope and fulfilment.

Think big picture. Act big picture. The hive needs you.

—Anna

Further Reading

Ashner, Laurie & Meyerson, Mitch, *When is Enough, Enough? What You Can Do if You Never Feel Satisfied*, Centre City, Hazelden, 1997

Astyk, Sharon, *Depletion & Abundance—Life on the New Homefront*, Gabriola Island, New Society Publishers, 2008

Berry, Wendell, *Bringing it to the Table—On Farming and Food*, Berkeley, Counterpoint Press, 2009

Carlson, Richard, *What About the Big Stuff?*, New York, Hyperion, 2002

Campbell, Colin, *The Coming Oil Crisis*, Essex, Multi-Science Publishing Co Ltd, 2004

Canfield, Jack, *The Success Principles—Get from Where You Are to Where You Want to Be*, New York, Harper Collins, 2005

Deveson, Anne, *Resilience*, Crows Nest, Allen & Unwin, 2003

Flannery, Tim, *Here on Earth: An Argument for Hope,* Melbourne, Text Publishing, 2010

Gardner, Howard, *Intelligence Reframed*, (New York: Basic Books, 2007)

Graham, John, *Stick Your Neck Out: A Street Smart Guide to Creating Change in Your Community & Beyond*, San Francisco, Berrett-Koehler Publishing, 2005

Greer, John Michael, *The Long Descent*, Gabriola Island, New Society Publishers 2008

Grille, Robin, *Parenting for a Peaceful World*, Woollahra, Longueville Media, 2005

Gritser, Greg, *Fat Land (How Americans Became the Fattest People in the World)*, New York, Houghton Mifflin Harcourt, 2003

Hamilton, Clive, and Denniss, Richard, *Affluenza*, Crows Nest, Allen and Unwin, 2005

Hamilton, Clive, *Requiem for a Species*, Washington, Earthscan, 2010

Heinberg, Richard, *The Party's Over—Oil, War and the Fate of Industrialised Societies*, 2nd edition, Gabriola Island, New Society Publishers, 2005

Heinberg, Richard, *Powerdown: Options & Actions for a Post-Carbon World*, Gabriola Island, New Society Publishers, 2004

Hopkins, Rob, *The Transition Handbook—From Oil Dependency to Local Resilience*, Devon, Chelsea Green, 2008

Irvine, Dr John, *Handbook for Happy Families*, Warriewood, Finch Publishing, 2003

Jacobsen, Rowan, *Fruitless Fall—the Collapse of the Honey Bee and the Coming Agricultural Crisis*, New York, Bloomsbury USA, 2008

Malkan, Stacey, *Not Such a Pretty Face*, Gabriola Island, New Society Publishers, 2007

Marinoff, Lou, *The Big Questions—How Philosophy Can Change Your Life*, New York, Bloomsbury Publishing PLC, 2004

Martin, Hans-Peter & Schumann, Harald, *The Global Trap: Globalization and the assault on prosperity and democracy*, New York, St Martin's Press, 1997

Martin, James, *The Meaning of the 21st Century*, London, Riverhead Trade, 2007

Mason, Colin, *The 2030 Spike: Countdown to Global Catastrophe*, Sterling, Earthscan Publications Ltd, 2003

McKibben, Bill, *Eaarth*, New York, Henry Holt & Company, 2010

Merkel, Jim, *Radical Simplicity,* Gabriola Island, New Society Publishers 2003

Morse, Suzanne W, *Smart Communities: How Communities & Local Leaders can Use Strategic Thinking to Build a Brighter Future*, San Francisco, Jossey-Bass, 2004

Napthali, Sarah, *Buddhism for Mothers*, Crows Nest, Allen & Unwin, 2003

Payne, Kim John, *Simplicity Parenting*, New York, Ballantine Books, 2010

Ripley, Amanda, *The Unthinkable—who survives when disaster strikes—and why*, New York, Three Rivers Press; Reprint Edition, 2009

Seligman, Martin, *The Optimistic Child*, New York, Mariner Books, 2007

Seligman, Martin, *Authentic Happiness*, New York, Random House, 2002

Seymour, John, *The Self-sufficient Life and How to Live it,* New York, DK Publishing, 2009

Shipard, Isabell, *How Can I Use Herbs in My Daily Life?*, Nambour, David Stewart, 2003

Shipard, Isabell, *How Can I Be Prepared with Self Sufficiency and Survival Foods?*, Nambour, David Stewart, 2008

Simmons, Matthew R, *Twilight in the Desert*, Hoboken, Wiley, 2006

Smith, Rick and Lourie, Bruce, *Slow Death by Rubber Duck*, Toronto, Knopf, 2009

Spigarelli, Jack A, *Crisis Preparedness Handbook*, Alpine, Cross Current Pub, 2002

Stein, Matthew, *When Technology Fails*, White River Junction, Chelsea Green Publishing, 2008

Suzuki, David, *The Sacred Balance*, Vancouver, Greystone Books, 2007

Wann, Dave, *Simple Prosperity*, New York, St Martin's Press, 2007

Acknowledgements

It takes about 50,000 bees to run a successful hive, and nearly the same number of humans to get a book published, I reckon! Grateful thanks to:

Rod Blatch, aka the Bee Man, an amazing, sweet and generous mentor with a heart of gold who introduced me to the world of the honey bee.

All the authors who have shared their passion for children, family, the environment, human health, ethics, permaculture, organics, biodynamics, living skills and philosophy in their works.

The regular people, farmers, leaders and scientists who have raised our awareness of the threats posed by climate change, synthetic chemicals, globalisation and over-consumption of resources. I thank you for your inspiration; without you, I wouldn't have been in a position to change my life and write this book.

Susie "Juice" Jones, Leanne Sheraton, Christine Beury, Nicole Hateley, Sean Bedggood, Geoff Strain, Hayes Van Der Meer, John Perfumo, Rada Kincade, Donna Carrier and the McCowan, Baseley, Stuart, Warriner, Tyrell, Lehane, Milliss-Smith, Nissen, Smith-Glimmerveen, Patz, Watkins, Hayes, Perkins, de Berg, George, Arnoux, Oldfield, McBride, Roberts, Tyack, Fardell, Futterlieb, Kramar, Voss, Kennedy and Brady clans—family and friends in demand, who always deliver.

The wonderfully warm-hearted sharers of knowledge, laughter and home-grown delights from Dyers Crossing Landcare, Great Lakes Seedsavers, Manning Valley Produce Cooperative, Gloucester (hello Trish & Evan from Talawahl Nursery!) and Nabiac Farmers Markets. There are way too many people to mention by name but you know who you are! I still might not know how to cook, but I sure know where to go for a good feed and good seed!

All our fabulous farmstay guests (or is that friends? ☺), school group visitors and fun bus tour folk, who along with Destination NSW, Manning Valley Tourism, Great Lakes Tourism, Mid North Coast Tourism, Hunter Business Centre, T-QUAL Grants, NSW Dept of Trade & Investment and operators like Mal from Tuncurry Coach Tours, Rod & Colleen Richards of Coach Holidays & Tours, Henryk from Holiday Coast Tours, Newcastle & Port Stephens Coaches, Hopkinsons, Hunter Valley Buses, as well as Emily and Billy from Island Palms Forster who all saw the big picture in our little farm.

Being part of a farm, a family and writing a book takes a lot of time, so to all the WWOOFers and HelpXers who have visited Honeycomb Valley Farm and enriched our lives no end, we thank you and continue to think of you! Especially to the gorgeous Emily Shelton and Louisa Rockcliffe from the UK, who helped launch the final draft in between chicken wrangling, scything and chasing the kids (goat and human!).

And our family could never forget the help, warmth, laughs and learning we enjoyed with the original Robin Rainer (Canada), Jade Elliot-Archer (UK), Craig & Courtney (NZ), Adele Lam (Hong Kong), Jennifer Hunter (UK), Adam Holding (UK), Lorna Newton (UK), Basile Fagot (France), Ann-Sophie Giron (France), Shaun McCowen (USA), Stefania Piacentin (Italy), Rowena Barthel (UK), Mari Ek (Finland), Constance Miloud (France), Manon Blaskovic (France), Heike Westphal (Germany), Leonie Bayer (Germany), Wong "Tan" Yee (China), Lau Yip Hang "Addy" (China), Sepp Felder (Canada), Maria Michel (Canada), Cara Grant (Canada), Tom Hunt

(UK), Stephanie Williams (UK), Zhou Linlin, Huang Donghao and Huang Xinyun (Singapore), Megan Marsh (US), Tegan Knight (UK), Hyeon "Joo" Kim (Korea), Ester Lee (Hong Kong), Hannah Tarrant (UK), Sarah Bienmueller (Germany), Simone Biesinger (Germany), Thierry Tournié (France), Catherine Derieux (France), Sean Walters (US), Troy Moore (US), Allison Mellier (France), Simon Embarck (France), Katerina Kulper (Germany), Mira Crillovich-Cocoglia (Austria), Winja Baumfried (Austria), Mirjam Crillovich-Cocoglia (France), Sophie Peirce (Australia), Lydia Beger (Germany), Henning Nitzsche (Germany), Lauri Oskari Pitkanen (Finland), Toni Ahola (Finland), Lena Schuchardt (Germany), Oliver Dahms (Germany), Virginie Belengri (France), Gene Doronila, (Canada), Gilles Fischer (France), Charles Duflo (France), Laure Bouvier-Verset (France) and the inimitable Phil and Netti Dalton (Australia). Thank you all—you hold a special place in our hearts, farm and family history. And to all the Wwoofers and HelpXers who came after this book was put to bed—we thank you too!

To the lovely librarians at Greater Taree City Library and Great Lakes Library, as well as Manning Valley Books, Great Lakes Book Shop and the Gloucester Bookshop, many thanks for the great service and wealth of knowledge you share. Also to Taree Scribblers who gave me the confidence to give this book a go and to some favourite cafés who provided much needed fuel after hours of writing: Raw Sugar, Wallamba, Bowers, Bent on Food and Greenhouse Cottage.

Editor Geoff Whyte, for editing and encouraging me to finally let this buzz loose on the world. He, along with Carolyn Crowther of Three60 Agency, and early assessors Diane Stubbings and Sean Doyle set me on the right flight.

Pat and Frank, who have known me, raised me, loved me, and made me—thanks for it all. I don't know if I could have had any shorter yet mightier parents!

Finally, to the complete and utter love of my life AC and our own very special sweet hive of three—you are all the bee's knees.

I love you around the universe and back times a gazillion (and add a gazillion more for good measure)! Fly high or wherever you like, enjoy the breeze! This love goes forever. ☺

Index

Join the conversation at
www.honeycombkidsparentingbook.com

Enjoy more information and purchase
additional copies of this and other books at:

www.capeable.com

Postal Orders:
Cape Able, PO Box 55, Nabiac NSW Australia 2312